PIONEERING PRINCIPLES

PIONEERING PRINCIPLES

By

JOHN THURMAN
Camp Chief, Gilwell Park

Publication Approved by
THE BOY SCOUTS ASSOCIATION, LONDON, ENGLAND
and published by
C. ARTHUR PEARSON, LTD.
TOWER HOUSE, SOUTHAMPTON STREET, LONDON, W.C.2

© JOHN THURMAN

First Published 1962

To Bill Campbell,
Deputy Camp Chief attached to Gilwell Park, whose help and
encouragement have enabled Gilwell to continue to pioneer.

Printed by Wm. Stevens, Ltd., York and bound by Key and Whiting, Ltd.,
London

CONTENTS

LIST OF PHOTOGRAPHS
(Between pages 64 and 65)

INTRODUCTION

THERE are few activities which, properly presented, have a greater appeal to the Scout and Senior Scout than Pioneering and ever since the introduction of Wood Badge training, Pioneering has been given a full share in the programme of Scouters' training. In the summer months when Scouters at Gilwell are building bridges, towers, and rafts, and boys are in camp it has been all too common to hear from the boys such remarks as, "I wish we did that in our Troop" or "We never do anything like that".

I said in the opening sentence "properly presented". This book is designed to help you, the Scouter, to plan and present Pioneering in a practical and effective way.

The main snags, I think, are:—

(a) Lack of knowledge and the consequent fear on the part of the Scouter,

(b) Lack of equipment,

(c) Lack of a suitable place where Pioneering can be carried out.

I hope that as the book evolves I shall be able to deal with all these problems and, indeed, I propose to return to them from time to time.

Let me say at the outset that Pioneering without preparation is no proposition for Scouting. Preparation always means thought, effort and work. Perhaps some of us forget that one of our continuing tasks is to provide the necessary facilities. Obviously, for some it is very difficult, but it is always possible to try. What I regard as unforgiveable is sitting back and saying, "We have no money; therefore we have no equipment: therefore we cannot do Pioneering."

Why Pioneering? To me the over-riding reason for presenting Pioneering is that boys like it. Some years ago we started providing simple equipment which Troops in camp at Gilwell can use. The demand is insatiable. Year by year we add more, but we never provide enough; because as one Troop sees another using the equipment and building a bridge they want to try it also and the desire to do Pioneering spreads like a contagious disease throughout the camp.

But there are reasons for Pioneering other than the fact that boys like doing it. B.-P. wrote: "I am inclined to suggest to Scouters that in addition to the technical details of knotting, lashing, and anchorages, there is an educative training in Pioneering since it gives elementary training in stresses, etc., and it also develops initiative and resourcefulness to use local material. Additionally, it gives practice in team work and discipline." In other words, Pioneering is practical and character building: the two essential ingredients of any programme material for Scouts.

The modern cynic may think it is all very old-fashioned but the short answer to this is, "Yes, of course it is, but so is breathing and sleeping and other things that mankind has been doing for a long time." It does not follow that because an activity has been used for a long time it is out-dated and, in fact, I am prepared to say that there is more interest in Pioneering today than ever before, perhaps because facilities have improved and perhaps because some of us have made an effort to present Pioneering to the Movement in a more imaginative and varied way. Quite apart from that, though, Pioneering is not old-fashioned in its purely technical sense.

I was showing a Managing Director of a large civil engineering firm round Gilwell when a Wood Badge Course was pioneering near the Bomb Hole. He displayed very great interest in the Pioneering and looked closely at all that was happening. From our point of view there was nothing unusual going on; this was a usual routine exercise with two or three bridges being built, a couple of towers, and a raft. As we walked away my civil engineering friend said, "I am delighted that the Scout Movement is still doing this: it is tremendously important. Despite the fact that modern machinery and equipment is magnificent there often comes a time when a man has to use ingenuity and improvise in order to move the job forward and the engineer who has the spirit that your kind of training produces is the man we want in our business."

Those of us who can think back to the war years remember with pride the Bailey Bridge and the Mulberry Harbour which, when you analyse them, were really nothing more than an imaginative extension of Boy Scout Pioneering.

Perhaps a final story at this point will not come amiss. Soon after the end of the war when we had the first German Scouters at Gilwell, I had just devised for the sheer fun of it a paddle steamer raft (which appears in "Pioneering Projects") and I watched with interest and amusement a young German Scouter who, seeing this monstrosity making its ungainly way around the Bomb

Hole, observed it closely and was obviously thinking very deeply. When he saw me watching him he turned and said, "Now I understand why Great Britain won the war." Taken aback, I replied, "What has this contraption to do with winning the war?" He smiled and said, "This thing is ridiculous, but it works!"

Well, that is Pioneering. It is good fun, practical, character training, and within the reach of every Troop if the Scouters will only make the effort.

Now what is this book all about, and why another book, anyway?

In the last ten years I have produced—and the Movement seems to like them—"Pioneering Projects" and "Fun with Ropes and Spars". These books are concerned primarily with individual projects. This book in a sense is more elementary: it replaces the old book "Preparing the Way: Pioneering" in the *Gilcraft* series, and it owes a great deal to the original compiler of that book. Why replace it then? Simply because I have a host of new ideas and a lot of experience that I have been lucky enough to gather from my visits overseas and from working at *Gilwell*, and, as I think you know, I like few things better than giving away ideas because I can give them to you and still have them for myself. This book, then, is up to date with all the basic skills, lashings, anchorages, etc., that are essential for effective Pioneering. Over and over again I see Troops start Pioneering in a muddle which often leads to ending in a muddle and probably also leads to ending in the middle of a stream.

The truth is that you cannot hope for success in a technical sense or in a character training sense unless you start by mastering the essentials, the knots and lashings, the choice of equipment, how to reeve a block, when to use a snatch block and when not to do so, how to choose a picket, drive it in, and get it out again, which way up to put an oil drum, and how to make an anchorage. Most of these things are simple in themselves, but cumulatively they are not only essential to good and enjoyable Pioneering but they are a terrific fund of experience gathered from Scouting and many other sources. Not least about most of the things I shall mention in this book; they can be learned and practised in the Troop Room, on a piece of waste ground, through the use of drawings and models and with a minimum of expense. They are things which, worked into the Troop programme, will bring a breath of the outdoor world into the Troop Meeting on a dull, dark, winter night. Some of them you can put into a display for a parents' evening and all of them are practical.

Finally, let me say this: There is not going to be a single theoretical suggestion in this book. Everything I shall write about I have either used myself or have seen somewhere in Scouting somewhere in the world. Therefore I am offering you a great deal of Pioneering experience that I have been lucky enough to gather as I have travelled the world on behalf of Scouting.

JOHN THURMAN,
Gilwell Park, 1962.

1

CORDAGE AND ROPES

THERE are two main aspects of cordage and ropes that I am going to attempt briefly to deal with:

    (1)   The selection of cord and ropes,

    (2)   The use of ropes.

Over the years I have received requests to devise Pioneering projects which require no blocks, no spars, and no ropes and, whilst I am greatly in favour of improvising, I have never been able to devise a satisfactory improvisation out of nothing at all!

It is worth remembering that ropes are in some senses artificial and have been manufactured. Several times when I have been running training courses in far distant countries where ropes are either too expensive or relatively unknown I have been impressed by the amount that can be achieved with completely natural materials; vines cut from the great trees in the jungle or strong grasses twisted to form a very satisfactory rope.

Adventure or Foolhardy?

The point I want to impress very firmly is that, whilst Pioneering should be an adventure, it is the duty of the leader—be he the Scoutmaster or any other adult—

to obviate the unnecessary hazards. It may be adventurous when the bridge collapses and the Scout is thrown into the stream but, equally, if the reason is bad equipment or bad elementary training then the leader has put the Scout in a position of unnecessary peril. This is a theme I shall inevitably return to several times in this book, but I want to get the point strongly across in the early stages. In a sentence:

The Scoutmaster is always responsible for the welfare of his Scouts and this is an even better reason than thrift for seeing that Pioneering materials are carefully selected and properly looked after, being checked for defects in some regularly systematic way.

We come, then, to a few thoughts about ropes; what is suitable and what is unsuitable.

Rope Material

The cordage and rope which we will for the most part use are made from sisal or manila hemp. Sisal comes from many parts of the world and is a vegetable material, as indeed, are all ropes except wire ropes or modern factory processed rope. A great deal of sisal comes from Mexico. Large amounts of manila come from the Philippines, hence its name. Cotton, particularly where a smart appearance is concerned, is another sound material from which rope is made. In recent years man-made fibres have made available nylon and Terylene ropes. At the time of writing these are expensive and there are still a few technical snags in terms of stretching and other strange behaviour when some of the established knots are used, but they are clearly a thing of the future and the Scout of today should be introduced to them.

All rope, whether natural or man made material, is made up by twisting fibres together and the stages are:

(1) Individual fibre twisted into thread,

(2) A number of threads twisted into yarn, (cord is made by twisting together a number of threads)

(3) Two or more yarns twisted together form a strand,

(4) Several strands—usually three—twisted together form a rope.

The Lay of Ropes

Observation comes into every Scout activity that I am familiar with and one of the things I would teach a Scout is to look at any rope and through his applied observation decide:

(a) what it is made of,

(b) how it is laid up,

(c) if there is anything unusual about it.

The most common lay of rope is three strands laid up from the bottom left to top right and this lay is known as Right Handed. A rope of three strands laid up right handed is called *Hawser laid*. Sometimes you will find four strands laid up right handed or four strands similarly laid round a heart or core. This is called *Shroud laid*.

For very heavy ropes it is usual to build them up by laying three hawser laid ropes together left handed and this is called *Cable laid*. It is generally accepted that hawser laid rope is strongest and, size for size, cable and shroud laid ropes are about 20% weaker. In Europe it is common for hawser and shroud laid ropes to be laid up left

handed but there is nothing significant in this and it
does not alter the strength of the rope, but it does mean
that we have to think out the process when we come to
splicing or undertaking any fancy rope work.

Now an answer to a rather ridiculous question but
one which I find Scouts ask fairly frequently:— If you
take a right-handed laid rope and turn it up the other
way is it still laid up right-handed? The answer is "Yes",
but don't just accept that; have a look for yourself.

I mentioned "size for size", and this brings us to our
next point:

The Measurement of Ropes

Ropes are normally described by their circumference
in inches.   Mathematicians will easily deduce, therefore,
that a 3 inch rope is just under 1 inch in diameter.
Incidentally, nothing smaller than this is ever referred
to as rope but as string or twine; and cord and line are
also usual terms. If you want a simple activity try working
different types of rope as a Kim's Game. Three questions
you can ask are "What is it made of?" "What is its lay?"
and "What is its size?"

The Strength of Rope

To return to this point about safety; we ought always
to plan our Pioneering in order to have a tremendous
safety margin.   The figures I give you are accurate but
when you are working with a vegetable material all
kinds of minor hazards can come in and I personally
would not dream of working in Pioneering unless the
safety margin was at least three times what the book
tells me it is:

The safe load.—The formula (and this applies primarily to hemp) is that the safe working load is equal in hundredweights to the square of the circumference in inches. Let's see if we can get at this in practical terms. A 3 in. rope (and remember that means three inches in circumference) would have a nine hundredweight safe working load and if, for example, you built a monkey bridge using a 3 in. rope as the foot rail, in theory the rope would take 9 cwts. of boy, (something better than a whole Patrol), but rope is strained with use and the older it is the less safe it becomes or, put another way, the safe working load reduces with age. It may comfort you to know that the figure I have given represents about one-sixth of the calculated breaking load but, nonetheless, watch it and the older a rope the more you must watch it.

The Weakening Effect of Knots

Because a knot looks and is strong it is often forgotten that any knot (and I do want to make it clear: any knot) weakens a rope considerably. A splice weakens a rope by 10—20%, a timber hitch by 25%, and a bowline by 40%, a reef knot or sheet bend by 50%, and an overhand knot by at least 55%. So you will understand that when you consider your safe working load you then have to consider the effect of the necessary knots to put the rope to the use you require and the safety margin will be reduced. So, again, you must watch.

Caring for Rope

I mentioned earlier that rope deteriorates with age. This is true of people also and, as with people, if we look after the health of the rope and see that it is properly housed we can preserve its strength for a much longer period than if we misuse it. I have often thought what a tremendous contribution to the rope-making industry the Scout Movement has made. Not only do we use miles of rope but we waste miles of it. I am familiar with the difficulties; the unsuitable storage place, packing up in a hurry, having no facilities for drying wet ropes, etc. All I can do is to give you advice which I know is sound:—

1. All ropes should be kept as dry as possible.

2. No rope should be coiled or put away when it is damp. Mildew, apart from being unpleasant to handle is not dis-similar in its effect to rust on metal. It will eat into the fibre and create a weakness, thereby being a danger.

3. Ropes should be laid in the shade to dry or be hung under cover and allowed to dry thoroughly before being coiled and put away.

4. Baking wet ropes in an oven is not recommended: it is true that it will dry the rope but it will also take the natural oils out of the fibres and perhaps weaken the rope even more.

5. Examine thick ropes from inside. I know that is difficult, but you cannot tell what is happening to a rope unless you open it and have a look at the inside of the strands. Obviously you will not look at every inch of the rope but check every six to eight feet of it.

6. Sometimes a rope cannot be properly looked after and it therefore gets very stiff and hard and is difficult to run through a block. It is reasonable to put a hard rope end into water and bring it to the boil but, having

done that, remember to stretch the rope and to dry it thoroughly. Technically I believe this process does weaken a rope but not appreciably; anyway, it can make an unserviceable rope serviceable once again.

7. A rope should always be coiled in the direction of its lay. This means that a hawser or shroud laid rope should be coiled clockwise and a cable or European laid rope should be coiled anti-clockwise.

8. The actual size of the coil must depend upon the storage facilities. Rope comes from the makers in tightly wound coils but it is hard, unnecessary, and perhaps even undesirable to coil in exactly the same way. I believe that the best way of coiling for most purposes is to stand with your back to the rope to be coiled and start the bottom of the coil one pace (your own pace) in front of you. Some people like to bring the rope from the side and others prefer to bring it between their legs, but it does not matter which is done. Coil the rope, standing at the bottom of the coil, and make the turns equivalent to your reach. When you have done this you will find that you have made a coil which can be carried on your shoulder without dragging on the ground and, consequently, it is easy to move about with it and is also easy for storage. Fix it with one piece of sisal or string with a loop in it for hanging and you will find that you have achieved your coiling effectively; the rope can dry easily if it is damp and, above all, it cannot get tangled—and that is important.

2

LASHINGS OLD AND NEW

IN this Chapter I am going to publish, I believe for the first time, two or three lashings that I have discovered in my travels abroad. I am not for one moment suggesting that they should take the place of the traditional lashings, but I am suggesting that, especially with Senior Scouts and Rovers, here is a new field of experiment and exploration. The lashings I shall introduce to you I have tried out and they have yet to fail: I am not just giving you an idea but the result of some very real experience.

Let me begin with this firm statement: Lashing is never a thing that you do in a hurry. I am all for knotting races, and with practice you can learn to be very quick indeed at tying almost any knot, but a lashing race is fundamentally unsound because a good lashing of any type must be done with great care and it must be tightened as it goes. I would go a stage further and say that when you are testing a Scout in Second Class or First Class lashing, never pass him unless he gets it exactly right. This is not a case where the effort matters more than the result; the effort has to lead to the correct result because somebody's limbs may one day depend upon the skill and experience of someone's second class lashing re-produced in action.

Perhaps this is an appropriate moment to suggest a rather different thought to you. Why do we expect a boy to learn the clove hitch? If your answer is, "So that he can pass a test" then I regard that as a very inadequate and short-sighted answer. I want a boy to learn the clove hitch so that he can use it to make a lashing and, having learned to make a lashing I want him to use the lashing to build a worthwhile Pioneering project which he will enjoy making and using. The sequence, I think, is this:—You learn the clove hitch so that you can make a lashing: you learn a lashing so that you can go Pioneering: you go Pioneering because you enjoy it.

To come back to slightly more mundane matters:—

Lashings are generally used to lash together two spars or poles. A lashing may be used to fasten a block or a drum to a spar. There are four traditional types of lashing and before I have finished this Chapter I hope to have added several more to the traditional types.

Square Lashing

This has nothing whatever to do with the angle at which the spars are set to each other. The spars can cross each other at any angle. The square lashing is used when, and only when, two spars crossing each other tend to lie together, never when they tend to fall away from each other.

The lashing begins with the clove hitch made round the most securely based spar. There are two common situations. The first is when a spar is driven into the ground and you want to lash a spar horizontally to it.

You would normally make the first clove hitch round the spar that is in the ground, and you would make the clove hitch below the horizontal spar. The other situation, which perhaps is more common, is when you are working on the ground and the piece of equipment, when finished, will be embodied in the whole project. In this case one spar will be on the ground and one spar will be above the first spar. Make your first clove hitch on the spar that is on the ground. There is an exception, which I will come back to later. Before you tie the first clove hitch always think how best it can be put to work; don't just tie it thoughtlessly. The clove hitch is stronger than any single turn in the lashing and so we might just as well make it work as merely let it hold. If, for example, the lashing is going to support the roadway to a bridge then the strain will be downwards, therefore, make your clove hitch at the point *below* the horizontal spar. If, however, the trestle you are making is to rest on the bed of a stream, then the strain will be upwards so you make the first clove hitch *above* the horizontal spar. This is making the hitch do as much work as possible.

Leaving enough free end.—A common mistake when tying the clove hitch is to leave too little free end. The best tied clove hitch can become untied unless the running end is sufficiently long to be twisted round the standing end before the lashing proceeds. I like six to twelve inches of running end for this winding round process but the actual amount depends upon the thickness of the lashing I am using.

The first turn.—I think you can follow from the sketches that, having made the clove hitch, the lashing is then taken in front of and over the top of the second spar, then behind the upright spar and

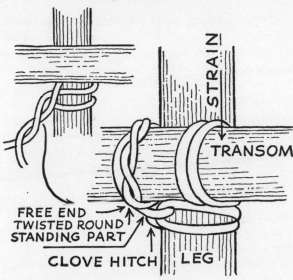

FREE END
TWISTED ROUND
STANDING PART

CLOVE HITCH LEG

STRAIN

TRANSOM

SQUARE LASHING

down in front of the second spar. Finally, it is taken behind the upright spar immediately above the original clove hitch.

This process is not very easy to describe, but it is easy to follow from the drawing. The one thing to remember is that every turn, and indeed every half turn, must tend to draw one spar on to the other.

The subsequent turns.—Having made one complete turn as described we then repeat the process, keeping on the *outside* of the first turn on the *horizontal* spar and *inside* the first turn on the upright spar. Some teachers of lashing advocate forced tightening after each complete turn and this can be effected by using an ordinary tent mallet, taking a half hitch round the handle of the mallet and using the mallet as a lever to get the turn as tight as possible. This is undoubtedly a sound and efficient method, but for a small boy it is a very difficult performance and you can get just as good results by banging in a few wedges when the whole of the lashing has been completed.

We have now completed two turns and, personally, I think one more is enough, i.e., three complete lashing turns. Some people prefer to use four turns and if the rope is available, there is no harm in putting on another turn. Make sure that at no point does one turn override another; if it does so it is a potential weakness, and this is where care and taking enough time becomes so important.

Frapping.—After three of four lashing turns we have to frap. Frapping is a method of drawing the running end two or three times round the lashing turns, i.e., between the spars. Pull the rope as tight as possible and the effect will be to secure the lashings.

The Finish.—Then comes the question of finishing off. The general advice (and I am sure it is good) is to finish off with a clove hitch round the spar other than the one on which you put the first clove hitch and to try to pull the clove hitch into the crevices from which the rope that starts the hitch takes off. Well, I have written it again and I have said it often, and I still find it difficult to get that second clove hitch in a position where it cannot slip.

One of the things I have learned over the years is that when something is really difficult there is no point in trying to "bludgeon" through; it is better to try to eliminate the difficulty. One of the lashings I give you later does eliminate this final clove hitch and, in fact, eliminates all clove hitches, so I hope that when you come to it you will like it.

There is one other thing to say about Square Lashing. When the job is completed to your satisfaction it is not a bad thing, if the spars are big and the lashing is thick, to beat the whole thing with a frapping mallet—not because you are annoyed with it but because you can beat the turns into the ideal position more easily than you can pull them into position.

Lastly, if there is a loose bit of lashing left over, finish it off neatly with a few additional hitches around the spar and the end tucked in.

Diagonal Lashing

This is used when two spars tend to spring apart. Again, it has nothing whatever to do with the angle at which the spars cross each other, there may be a wide angle or it may be that one spar is set at an angle of 90° to the other. If, from the nature of the construction, they tend to spring apart as, for example, the braces in a trestle, then the diagonal lashing is correct. Perhaps it puts it into focus if I say that you can always use a diagonal lashing even when you would normally use a square lashing, but you must not use a square lashing when the diagonal lashing should be used. So you will realise that the diagonal lashing is the more important of the two.

Start with a Timber Hitch.—The essence of this lashing is that it starts with a timber hitch, a knot which itself will tend to pull the two spars together. Firmly tied, even with no additional turns, a timber hitch can serve as a sound emergency lashing. It is a knot where the greater the strain the better it holds;

its danger is only when there is no strain, and it can then fall apart. Even so you can secure a timber hitch by working a clove hitch on to it.

So, we start with a timber hitch round the two spars, and here the argument is likely to start. Where do we go from there? Some schools say "Follow the timber hitch round for three turns and then reverse and make three turns round the other fork." The other school says, "It goes round the fork opposite to the line of the timber hitch and then goes back and follows the timber hitch." I have tried both ways and I do not believe there is much difference technically, but for neatness the first way is better. Frapping turns are taken as before, gripping the lashing and running between the spars. Finish with a clove hitch on a convenient spar.

Sheer Lashing, Mark I

This is sometimes called a Round Lashing but is more commonly called "sheer", and the spelling is as I have put it and not shear! Mark I is for forming sheer legs and this is the one type of lashing which you *must not* artificially tighten, for the simple reason that when you open the sheer legs that action in itself will tighten the turns. If you artificially tighten them you cannot open the sheer legs and, indeed, if you use sufficient force you must break the lashing, and that doesn't achieve anything!

How to start.—Start this lashing with a clove hitch round *one* spar; which one doesn't matter: I repeat *one* spar, never round both.

The lashing turns.—Take eight or ten turns at whatever point is suitable, bearing in mind how much "top" you want to the sheer legs when they are opened.

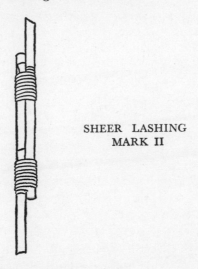

SHEER LASHING
MARK II

Frapping.—Having made the turns, firmly but not too tightly, frap twice by taking turns between the two spars and going round the lashing turns, finishing with a clove hitch on the spar opposite to the one where you put the first clove hitch and preferably at the opposite end of the lashing.

Turns can be too tight.—A common fault in making this lashing is to make the turns too tight and to find that you cannot get the frapping turns between the spars so, personally, unless I am working with very small material of, say, Scout staff size, I put a small block of wood between the spars before I start the lashing and then I know there will be adequate room for the frapping turns and I save a lot of blood, sweat, and skin as a result.

Well, that is Sheer Lashing Mark I and so we move to Sheer Lashing Mark II.

Sheer Lashing, Mark II

This is a very different fellow.

Its purpose.—Here we are going to extend the length of a spar by lashing another spar to it and so we want the utmost rigidity. You cannot achieve success in this instance unless you have:

(*a*)   a good overlap between the spars (I recommend a minimum of a quarter of the length of each spar but one-third is better) and,

(*b*)   two sheer lashings as the drawing (on page 27) shows.

How to start.—Most of the books say "Start with a clove hitch round both spars". I agree because that is all right, but I have found from experience that starting with a timber hitch is even more effective, especially if I remember to take the running end, after I have completed the timber hitch, into the first couple of turns of the lashing. In any event, the knot goes round *both spars*: that is the vital thing. I then take eight or ten turns as in Mark I and I finish with a clove hitch (not a timber hitch this time) round both spars or round one.

No frapping.—There are no frapping turns because all they would do in this case is to weaken the lashing you have made; they cannot possibly strengthen it in this position. If there is any sign of weakness, and there may be if the spars are uneven with knots in the wood, etc., then I tighten the lashing by driving in wooden wedges (not lumps of iron).

So Sheer Lashing Mark II is really something on its own, and the Scout needs to distinguish one sheer lashing from the other and to be competent to make both.

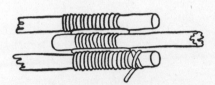

FIGURE OF EIGHT LASHING

Figure of Eight Lashing

So we come to the Figure of Eight Lashing which is used to lash three poles together in order to form a tripod or "gyn". Lay the three spars together so that the end of the centre spar points in the opposite direction to the ends of the outer spars. The lashing starts with a clove hitch around one of the outside spars at a reasonable distance from the end. Six or seven turns are then taken quite loosely round the spars, working under and over alternately, like a figure of eight. The lashing is finished off with *loose* frapping turns and a clove hitch on the other outside spar. If the lashing is too tight it will not be possible to bring the legs to form an equilateral triangle on the ground.

An Alternate Way

Here is another and quicker way of lashing poles together in order to form a tripod, if the tripod is not to be used for supporting heavy weights.

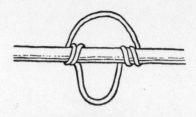

LASHING   A   BLOCK
TO   A   SPAR

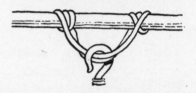

Hold the poles in a vertical position, butts on the ground. Lay the end of the lashing along one of the poles and tightly wrap the other end of the lashing three or four times round the poles, winding from the tip downwards and binding the first end laid against the pole. Now carry the free end upwards over the wrappings, and then downward underneath the wrapping as shown in the drawing. Pull this end down and jamb it tight between the wrappings and one of the poles. When the butts of the poles are spread this lashing will hold firm.

Lashing a Block to a Spar

Begin with a clove hitch round the spar above the block, taking the lashing two or three times round the spar and the hook of the block, and finish off with a clove hitch round the spar below the block.

Using a Strop

Another method is to use a strop—an endless rope formed by means of a short splice. This is passed round the spar and through its own bight, the purchase on the block keeping the strop in place. If the spar is not very thick, or if you wish to secure a block to a rope, a longer strop is used. The middle of the strop is placed against the rope, and cross turns taken until the bights come together, when the hook of the block is put through them.

Japanese Square Lashing

So far as I know this is the first time this lashing has appeared in print, at any rate in this country. Why Japanese? For the good and sufficient reason that I first saw this lashing when I was running a Training Course in Japan. As a matter of fact, I am not even sure that it was shown to me by a Japanese, but that is beside the point: so far as I am concerned it will always be the Japanese Lashing, and that seems as appropriate a name as any.

You will remember that when I was writing about Square Lashing I mentioned my failure (which I believe is shared by all honest practitioners of lashing) to get the second clove hitch to lock with certainty where the books say it should. You may remember also that I said that one of my approaches to any problem was to see if the cause of the problem could be eliminated. The wonderful thing about the Japanese lashing is that it does eliminate the second clove hitch and, for that matter, it eliminates the first clove hitch as well. The only knot involved is the reef knot.

JAPANESE
LASHING

START

JAPANESE
LASHING

FIRST STAGE

JAPANESE
LASHING

FRAPPING
TAKE OFF

JAPANESE
LASHING

COMPLETED

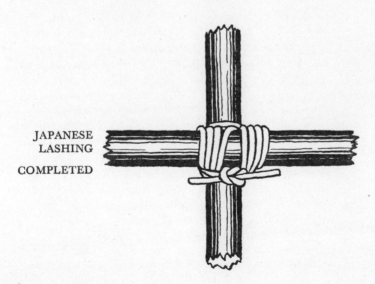

Like all lashings, it is easier to acquire the skill when it is shown to you than by reading about it but, whilst I shall continue to demonstrate lashings on all training courses, it inevitably takes a long time to reach a wide audience. After demonstration, good photographs and drawings are next in order of merit, and I hope and believe that the photographs between pages 64—65 plus my explanation of the pictures, will enable you to work out the procedure. I have been lucky to have the skilled photographic assistance of Bob Herbert.

How to start.—(no knot - not even mirrors)! You may have wondered what we are going to start with if not with the clove hitch, and the somewhat surprising and true answer is "With no knot at all". You take an ordinary lashing, preferably one about 30% longer than you would use for the traditional square lashing, and you use it as a double rope. Begin by passing the bight (which forms automatically if you halve the rope) round the lower spar and then with the two parts of the lashing side by side and never over-riding take two complete turns round both spars as for square lashing.

How to Frap.—Then take the two parts of the double rope and make frapping turns by taking the two ropes between the spars in opposite directions. One of the great advantages is that it is easier to pull these frapping turns really tight, far tighter than when you are pulling round in one direction only, and you have the added power of the two ropes pulling against each other.

How to Finish.—Two or three frapping turns are sufficient and then you finish the lashing by joining the two running ends together with a reef knot, tucking in the ends, and the job is done.

I am prepared to back the Japanese lashing against any square lashing. I am satisfied that it is more secure and I believe it is easier to tie, so have a shot at it and don't be worried if the first two or three times when you come to the point of starting the frapping turns you are slightly puzzled, I was but I was being shown in Japanese!

The discovery of the Japanese lashing led me to think and explore further and it was not very long before I was shown a different method of diagonal lashing. This is where the great virtue of giving away ideas pays such handsome dividends. I was demonstrating the Japanese lashing on a training course when there stepped forward a Scouter from the Boy Scouts of the Philippines who announced that he thought he could show me a different way of doing the diagonal lashing. Therefore, following the precedent, I hereby name the new diagonal lashing:—

The Filipino Diagonal Lashing

This is illustrated for you on the next page. Once again, there is no knot at the start of the lashing, and once again we use a double rope. Start by working the two ends of the lashing through the bight of the rope and, as with a timber hitch, use that device to draw the two spars together. Then follow round as with the traditional diagonal lashing. Two turns in one direction is sufficient and then reverse the turns through the opposite angle and then, as for the Japanese lashing, divide the ropes and frap, the two ropes going in opposite directions between the spars. Finish with a reef knot.

This is a quick, simple lashing and the advantage

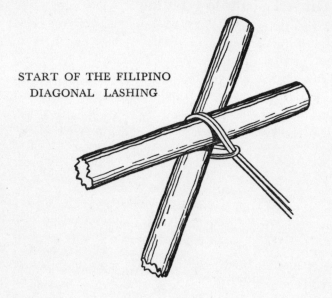

START OF THE FILIPINO
DIAGONAL LASHING

is that once again you have eliminated that final suspect clove hitch.

Don't use these two new lashings at the expense of learning the traditional lashings, but get your Scouts and yourself to add to your store of knowledge. You will do more efficient Pioneering if you have a variety of skills. See photographs between pages 64—65.

The next lashing I hardly know what to call. I am not claiming any originality for it as I am sure it must be used in the building trade but whatever we call it (and I hope you will not mind if, for the moment, I call it the Gilwell Scaffold Lashing) it is one I can commend to you, particularly if you are working with heavy spars.

The Gilwell Scaffold Lashing

If you have done any Pioneering at all you must have faced the difficulty of trying to lash one spar to another, possibly in a position high above the ground, when you obviously needed another arm, i.e., two hands to do the lashing and one hand to hold the horizontal spar in place. The problem is to make one spar secure to another before you have actually completed the lashing. Following the line of thought about eliminating the difficulties my thinking resulted in this: Why wait until I have done all the lashing turns before I put on any frapping turns? So, I experimented.

The Gilwell Lashing is simply this: Start in the

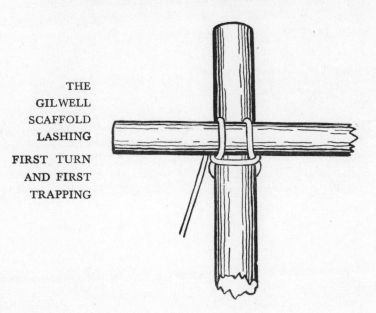

THE
GILWELL
SCAFFOLD
LASHING

FIRST TURN
AND FIRST
TRAPPING

orthodox way as for square lashing but, having made one set of lashing turns, *put on one frapping turn.* Providing you don't lose the end of the rope this does hold the spars together and they cannot slip; you are therefore free to continue work in the traditional way. Put on a second lashing turn *followed by a second frapping turn,* followed by a third lashing turn and a final frapping turn, and finish with a clove hitch as in the square lashing.

I admit that this lashing looks a little clumsy because the turns do not fit neatly together, but in my estimation it is definitely stronger and consequently is more efficient, and in Pioneering it is worth sacrificing a little beauty for added strength. In addition, it is easier to tie except when you are working flat on the ground; you have more control over the spars when using this lashing than when using the traditional square lashing.

The Tourniquet Lashing

This will shock the purists, but I am unrepentant.

Imagine a big Scout Rally with the main attraction publicised all over the town: "Pioneering Display". If the publicity has been good along comes the public, the Mayor and Corporation, and the mums and dads. The order is given; the Scouts rush on carrying a tremendous assortment of ropes and spars. Expectation is very great. The Scouts start work with a will and they try very hard, but the minutes and the half-hours pass and all over the arena Scouts of various sizes are putting on square lashings, diagonal lashings, and possibly other lashings as well—and they are probably enjoying doing it. But the audience cannot really see what is happening and the expectation of the crowd subsides gradually into

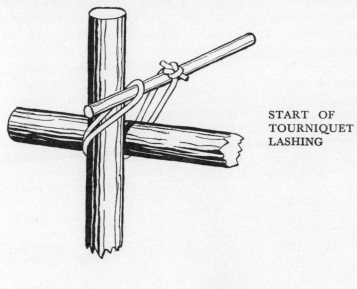

START OF
TOURNIQUET
LASHING

TOURNIQUET
LASHING IN
PROGRESS

the boredom associated with any English summer after-
noon when much has been promised and little is being
achieved. The spectators remember pressing engage-
ments, the Mayor begins to look at his watch, the District
Commissioner becomes increasingly harassed and runs
out of small talk. The Scoutmaster in charge knows
that Lashing should not be hurried and yet wants to
hurry it. Eventually the project or projects appear,
but too late; no one is really interested now but thinking
of tea and gardens. They have been kept waiting too
long. Not an imaginary picture I assure you—I've
seen it—I expect you have too.

How can we overcome a situation like this? The
thing that is taking the time is the lashing, the most
important and the least spectacular part of any enterprise
in Pioneering. Well, there can be a certain amount of
pre-lashing so that for the final erection of the bridge
or the tower a very small number of lashings have to be
put on (remember the bridge in "Boy Scout" at the
Albert Hall), but even this can take a long time. That
is why I commend to you for display work the Tourniquet
Lashing. It is my own idea and I don't think you will
find it in any other book. As I said earlier, I am sure it
will shock many people, but I hope it may shock some
of you into trying it. It is illustrated on the previous
page, and it does work!

Take a simple strop and then with a mallet handle
or the butt of a stave you can fix two spars together by
using the process of a tourniquet. Unless you are going
to have a Scout holding the strainer of the tourniquet
(an unpopular assignment) you must have a loop of rope
or a piece of sisal, as shewn in the drawing, to fix it in
place after tightening. Use this method for display
purposes and I promise you that with a little practice

you can put on a Pioneering Dislay that really does come up to expectations.

This is the method advocated in "The Ten-Minute Tower" which you will find described later in this book.

This leads to the final lashing suggestion, which will bring us to the end of a long but very important chapter and one which I hope you have found useful.

A great many valuable commercial discoveries have emanated from the thought of how to use something for a purpose for which it was not intended. Something is invented for one purpose and then ingenuity finds a different use for it. In lashing I cannot offer anything very profound except the tourniquet lashing and now this.

See photographs between pages 64—65.

The Sailmaker's Lashing

Anyone concerned with rope work knows that the Sailmaker's Whipping is a very good whipping for the end of a rope. It is simple to do, is a solid and secure job, and it looks attractive. Now, if it can be used for a three-stranded rope, why should it not be used for lashing together three spars? Through that process of reasoning we have been able to create the Sailmaker's Lashing.

I am not going to describe it in detail because the Sailmaker's Lashing is simply the whipping done on the end of three spars instead of the end of a three-stranded rope; there is no difference in method or result except perhaps to say that if you are putting on the lashing in order to make a tripod it must not be put on as tightly as would be done for a whipping. This is the same effect as in a sheer lashing: the tightening process occurs when you open out the spars and if you have made it too tight

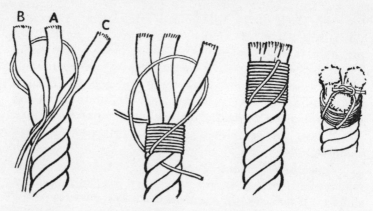

SAILMAKER'S WHIPPING

the only answer to the problem is to take it off and start again.

A further set of photographs (between pages 64—65) shows you the Sailmaker's Whipping as used on a four-stranded rope, and the same principle can be used for lashing four poles together, You may not want to do this very often, but it is as well to know that it can be done.

Lashing Lengths

It is useful to have some sort of formula as to the length of lashing rope required and also the desirable relationship between the thickness of the rope used and the thickness of the spars to be lashed. It is worth saying, however, that perfectly secure lashings can be made when the length and thickness of rope does not coincide with the formula and we must be prepared to improvise and on occasion to use material that is different to the ideal.

The old formula which we have used in Scouting for many years is that one fathom of lashing is required for every inch of the diameter of the thicker spar, and this is still a fair guide but recently at Gilwell we have put it under test and we can now help you even more. This "fathom to the inch" formula gets progressively out of proportion as the size of the spars increase and it takes no account whatever of the very common situation where you need to lash a relatively thin spar to a thick one, hence our experiments and this rather more exact formula.

I would commend to you this: *One yard of lashing for each inch of the diameters of the two spars together.* Put simply: If you are lashing a one inch spar to a four inch spar then you need five yards of lashing.

In considering the question of the thickness of the rope to be used our experience encourages me to say that with staves and spars up to $1\frac{1}{4}$ in. in diameter use codline; for between $1\frac{1}{4}$ in. and 3 in. use $\frac{7}{8}$ in. lashing and for spars over 3 in. use $1\frac{1}{4}$ in. lashing. As the thickness of the spars increases and consequently the formula asks you to use more rope you will find that you have a little more rope than is necessary, but this I regard as a much better error in formula than giving you one which leaves you with too little rope. It is easy enough to take an extra turn or two or to make fast with additional half hitches, but it is difficult to produce an essential frapping turn or fasten it off with no rope at all; that becomes conjuring and not Pioneering!

Put simply:—

1. For staves and spars up to $1\frac{1}{4}$ in. use codline.
2. For spars up to 3 in. use $\frac{7}{8}$ in. lashing.
3. For spars over 3 in. use $1\frac{1}{4}$ in. lashing.

In every case allow one yard of lashing for the *combined* diameters in inches of the spars to be lashed.

THE TEN MINUTE TOWER

This is a book about Pioneering principles and not one devoted to Pioneering projects. Most of you who read this book will be familiar with "Pioneering Projects", "Fun with Ropes and Spars" and "Pioneering for the Patrol" and it may be that some time in the future I shall be able to collect together sufficient material to be able to offer further ideas and adventures in the Pioneering field, but I do want you to know about this particular project because it links up so well with much that I say in this book about various principles, some of them new and some of them long established. Particularly do I commend the Ten Minute Tower for display purposes and for its versatility.

Let me make it clear, however, that you will not build the Ten Minute Tower in ten minutes the first time you attempt it, but it can be built in ten minutes (and indeed, the record so far as I know is just under nine minutes) provided that the Patrol has practised, is trained, is well led, and works as a team. I commend the tower to you as one of the best exercises in the practical working of the Patrol System that I think has yet been devised.

Obviously, the tower can be built in material of any size from Scout staves upwards, and I suppose it could be built with match sticks or pencils although I think that would take much longer.

It may help if I give you some idea as to how long I think a reasonably raw Patrol should take, assuming that they know their lashings—and if they don't know them they will never complete the job at all. I think anything under twenty minutes at the first attempt would be good, and the time ought to be less by two or three minutes at each subsequent attempt until eventually it can be built in just under ten minutes.

You will note from the drawing that there are points where the Tourniquet lashing is used, points where the Square Lashing or Japanese Lashing are used, and points where the Filipino Lashing is used. Finally, we have to use some form of Figure of Eight Lashing where the three spars come together.

This kind of project, apart from being a good exercise, is perfect for display purposes. It is something that really can be built quickly, and with a few boards placed on the top, within ten minutes the whole Patrol can be standing proudly on the top receiving, I hope, the applause of the astonished multitude.

If you want to be ambitious it is not difficult to build a high tower by mounting a slightly smaller Ten Minute Tower on top of the first one. A third structure built in still smaller material can be added safely, although you will need to use guys by this time. I have not seen any Patrol put four towers on top of each other, but there would be no harm in trying although you really would need to watch the guying.

The material required is obvious from the drawing, and about the method of construction I am only going to make two points:—

Good leadership ensures that the Patrol, working in pairs, is always kept busy and, in fact, if they are going to achieve the ten minute limit they must all be kept busy. As the pairs of Scouts make the various sections, the leader brings them together, completes the final lashings, and slips the top binding spars into place.

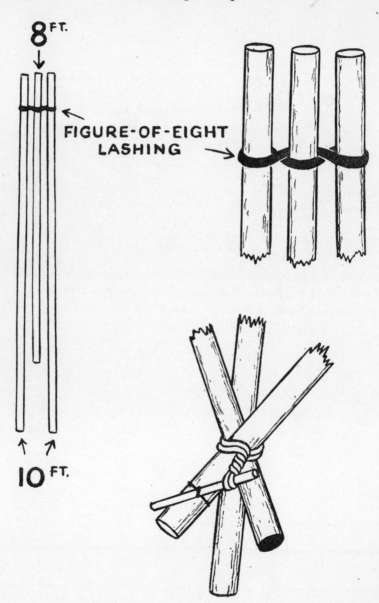

8 FT.

FIGURE-OF-EIGHT LASHING

10 FT.

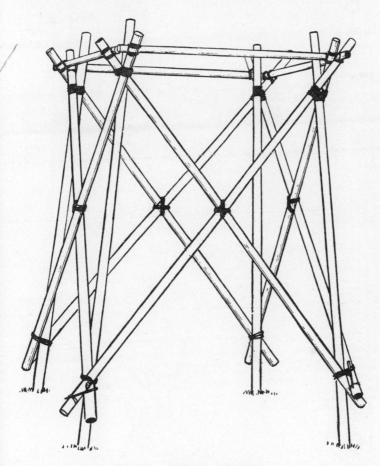

TEN MINUTE TOWER

The success or failure of the project (except the obvious one that it does not fall when built) is that when it is completed the top horizontal spars are parallel to the ground: in other words, can you have a level platform?   If you cannot then it may be very entertaining but it is not an efficient piece of Pioneering.

Finally for this chapter just a few reminders. Lashing requires these attributes:—

1.   Good equipment.
2.   A sure knowledge of which lashing to use.
3.   Regular practice.
4.   Thoroughness.
5.   No sacrifice of accuracy for speed.

3

ANCHORAGES

THERE is nothing connected with Pioneering that of itself is so important as the correct anchoring of a bridge or a tower. Quite apart from the fact that an insecure anchorage is a source of danger and therefore an avoidable hazard, it is a disappointing experience for a Patrol to work for two or three hours to erect something which they hope to enjoy using only to find that it collapses as soon as it is used, simply because they did not know how to secure it to the ground. It is true that the Scout spirit on occasion survives this sort of disaster and I shall always remember when I was running a Training Course at Pennant Hills in Australia, through inadequate anchoring a bridge collapsed. The Patrol Leader ran straight up to me, came smartly to the alert, saluted, and said, "I have to report our bridge prematurely dismantled." This was a fine spirit but not very good Pioneering.

Before I attempt to describe the different types of anchorages there are a few general matters I suggest you read and digest:—

Why do we have different types of anchorage? Could there not be one anchorage devised to serve all purposes? The answer is "no" for what is suitable in one situation is not so suitable or, indeed, may be quite unsuitable, in another. The first thing you have to consider is what kind of soil the anchorage is going to be put into. You must know and understand "the nature of the beast". An anchorage which suits the heavy clay of Gilwell Park will not work in light sandy soil, in marshy ground, or in solid rock. You will obviously (or you should) know the type of soil around your own area, but if you are doing your Pioneering elsewhere and do not know "the nature of the beast" you will have to test the ground and find out, driving in a picket here and a picket there, and trying the picket under strain to see if it really does hold. If it does not hold then you must use some other type of anchorage, and that is where I hope this chapter is going to help you.

The next point to consider is the difference between a natural anchorage and a man-made anchorage. This chapter is concerned mostly with the latter, but there is no reason at all why one should not use what nature has provided, be it a rock or a tree or something else that is convenient for the job we want to do.

I cannot claim to have a great deal of experience of anchoring into rock, but such experience as I have leads me to say that, here again, you must know the "nature of the beast". For example, a wire hawser fixed round a lump of soft lime stone is not going to provide a secure anchorage as the hawser will cut into and possibly through the rock. A lump of granite precariously balanced on a slope may easily start to slip if a strain is put upon it. There are occasions when the only answer is to drill into the rock and to fix permanent hold-fasts in concrete in the drilled holes, but this you would do only on a permanent site where you were going to do a lot of Pioneering. There are many sites in the world which I have visited where that has had to be done. If you have that sort of site then good quality ring bolts cemented into the rock are the right answer.

A much more familiar situation is to have trees readily accessible to the Pioneering site, and this is where we begin to see, and I hope teach, the virtue of a knowledge of woodcraft in relation to Pioneering. Yet again, you have to know the "nature of the beast" and be able to recognise a tree in Summer or Winter (which enables me to say that those who teach tree recognition only by leaves have gone only a very short way along the road of tree recognition).

In terms of anchorages there are many trees which are unreliable and which have to be avoided. In general these are most, but not all, trees which grow near water. For example, the willow tends to be shallow-rooted and it splits very easily. If you anchor to even a stout branch of willow it is liable under strain to tear away from the main trunk. The Alder, a water loving tree, in my experience is better than the willow but it also is shallow rooted and will not be safe if any real strain is put upon it. Any tree which grows out of rock is almost bound to be shallow-rooted, certainly so far as its main tap root is concerned. Most dead trees must be avoided, but not all; a dead oak, unless it is hollow, is an exception for that can be as sturdy as a living oak. The boughs of elm trees are notoriously brittle, and I would also say the same about lime trees. Young conifers (and by young I mean under thirty years) on the whole are unreliable. Indeed, if you look at the matter the other way round, from our knowledge of the splitting properties of woods, I think it is fair to say that any wood which splits easily is a dubious prospect as an anchorage.

All that I have said so far is very general, and so we move on to the particular forms of man-made anchorage. The majority of them require pickets, so we might begin with a little advice on bad *PICKETS*. The best wood in Great Britain for pickets is Sweet Chestnut. In many parts of the country it coppices well and therefore is reasonably inexpensive: it is straight, long-lasting, and does not split easily. Pickets need to be at least four feet long and preferably between four and five feet long, and about 4 in, in diameter. I would not trust a picket under 3 in. in diameter. It is worth taking the trouble to put a wire whipping on the end which is not going into the ground. (This is a good service for Rover Scouts: to make and equip pickets for the Troop). The pickets should be pointed at one end and the point be hardened by firing. Pickets thus selected and prepared will see you through a considerable number of Pioneering operations and if they are properly stored and kept clean they will last for several years. Shoddy, hastily made pickets are no use. Rule out straight away pickets made from all conifer trees, Silver Birch, Elm, and Willow.

For those who know the technicalities, here is the mathematical theory of pickets:—

A 3 in. diameter picket driven three feet into the ground will take a strain of seven hundredweights; a two and one hold fast will take a ton, and a three and two hold fast will take two tons.

All pickets and anchorages should be exactly aligned to the line of strain.

So much for the general; now to the particular:—

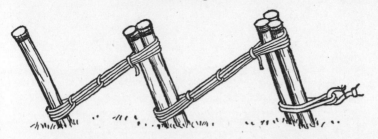

THE THREE TWO ONE HOLD FAST

Single Picket Anchorage

We know its capacity: not more than seven hundred-weights. In very heavy holding ground such as solid clay, it can adequately support a tower or the sheer legs of a monkey bridge, but I would regard it as inadequate and therefore hazardous in loose soil, in support of an aerial runway, or in support of anything where I expected the strain to be considerable. The single picket I would use, but use seldom.

The angle at which to set it is about 60° to the ground. It should slant away from the object it is anchoring.

The Two and One Hold Fast

Two pickets driven side by side supported by one picket to the rear. Its potential is considerable and we know it to be a ton. From near the top of the two pickets we take a lashing to near the foot of the single picket. The angle between the lashing and the picket should be 90°, and the pickets at 60° to the ground.

The Three Two One Hold Fast

In the right soil conditions this is about the strongest anchorage you can build; three pickets nearest the object

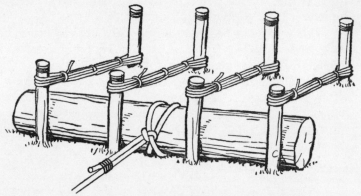

THE LOG AND PICKET HOLD FAST

you are anchoring, supported by two and supported again by one.   Strength: Two tons.   As in the Two and One lashing from the top of one ᴌet to near the base of the next.

Make sure that the rope lashings are a little above the ground. If you are building a Pioneering project and taking it down again almost immediately it will not matter, but if it is going to stay up for a few days then don't let the rope have the chance to absorb water from the ground and, equally, give the rope a chance to shed any rain water on to the ground. A small point, but good Pioneering is made up of small points.

The Log and Picket Hold Fast

This is very easily made. The theoretical strength is twelve hundredweights for every pair of pickets. You will see from the illustration that the first requirement in addition to the pickets is a good heavy log which should be placed directly at right angles to the line of strain. Fasten a strop round the log and fix the straining rope to the strop. Try to avoid fixing the straining rope direct to the log as this is inefficient.

It is worth taking the top spit off the ground immediately under the resting place of the log as it does add strength and prevents the log riding up the pickets. In this anchorage the pickets are often put in almost upright, although I personally prefer the supporting pickets to be set slightly at an angle. It will be obvious that we must have the same number of pickets on each side oj the straining rope.

In this anchorage and, indeed, in most, a very common failing is to put the anchorage too close to the project. The angle between the ground and the straining rope should never be more than 30°.

This log and picket hold fast can be used in heavy soil as the three-two-one, but it is particularly valuable in marshy ground or in any situation where it is desirable to spread the load and consequently the risk.

Dead Man's Anchorage

This is a semi permanent affair. We bury a heavy weight such as a log or a rock, and with a secure strop round that dead weight we have something really solid on which to anchor. It is almost as though we had a little man under the ground holding the rope for us. A channel should be made from the "dead man" to give the straining rope a true line and so that it does not have to cut over a corner. I would strongly recommend using a wire strop instead of a rope, particularly if the anchorage is going to be used for any length of time, and do remember that half the security of the Dead Man's Anchorage is the tamping down of the ground over the dead man, making it as hard and firm as you can manage.

From a very exciting but hazardous personal experience I can assure you that it is not just the weight of the dead man that matters. I was invited to try an aerial runway that some Scouts had built on a playing field. They assured me that they had a splendid Dead Man's Anchorage and, indeed, they thought they had. They had buried the cricket ground roller and had covered it well with earth. It had a proper strop on it and the straining rope was correctly fastened to the strop. As I came down the runway my weight was sufficient to make the roller mobile and out of the ground it rose, looking like some prehistoric beast. It is bad enough when a runway collapses and you come down with a nasty bump, but when, in addition, there is a half-ton roller advancing upon you it is a moment to remember and one to avoid repeating. So make sure that your "dead man" is really dead.

Spanish Windlass

This is a rather crude but very effective way of straining or tightening a slack rope.

One end of a rope is made fast to the load, and the other to a fixed hold, such as a tree or other suitable anchorage. A short, stout spar is then held by one Scout vertically against the centre of the rope, while a second fellow takes a smaller spar, and inserting it in a bight on the rope, as shown on the next page, walks round the upright spar, upon which both standing and running parts of the rope are wound as the upright spar approaches the fixed anchorage. The second, or hand-spar, must be kept above the turns of the rope. The amount of rope which can be wound up is limited, and it is advisable to take up the slack and make a fresh start at intervals, if the distance the load has to be moved is considerable. This obviously does not apply if you are using the windlass to tighten a fixed rope.

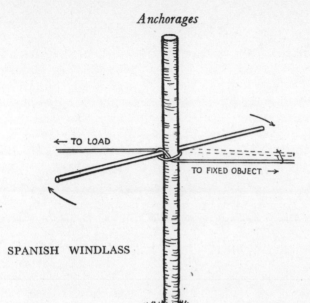

← TO LOAD

TO FIXED OBJECT →

SPANISH WINDLASS

When a Spanish windlass is used for tightening up the hawser of a ropeway, it is only a temporary expedient and should not be used on ropes that are to take a great weight, as it weakens the rope considerably. In this case it is possible to drive the first spar into the ground, and to lash the second spar to the rope to keep it in position when sufficient strain has been obtained.

This appliance is best reserved for Senior Scouts, as it must be used with great care. The principle employed is the same as in the Roman ballista, and the tension is quite sufficient to break a leg if the second spar, or windlass, is suddenly released. Make positive that no one, except the two strong fellows engaged on the job are anywhere near the windlass, that it is lashed very securely when under strain, and that every precaution is taken when the windlass is unlashed in order to lessen the strain.

5

GETTING ACROSS

CROSSING theoretical streams marked out by pieces of string is a perfectly legitimate and for many an inevitable exercise, but it naturally lacks reality and it does lead to the temptation to wander about in mid-stream which would be impossible if a real stream was there. Consequently, we have to learn how to get a line across and then to get equipment from one side of the stream to the other if we are going to give Pioneering the realism it deserves. When we have to use an artificial stream at least let us discipline ourselves and our Scouts by saying, "We will start from this side of the stream and we will evolve a genuine means of getting the gear across the stream to the other side which does not necessitate walking across the stream." Having said that, I know all too well the difficulties involved and, in fact, it is relatively simpler to transport gear across a real stream than across an imaginary one, but the important point at this stage is to resolve to play fair, otherwise when we come face to face with reality we just do not know how to cope.

Methods of getting across. In most practical situations I think it is perfectly reasonable to assume that one Scout can get across to the other side of the stream in some way or other, possibly by making a detour and going over a permanent bridge, possibly by swimming, possibly by using a raft. The function of the Scout on the opposite side to the main party is to catch and secure the line or rope which is sent across to form the transport basis. It should not be necessary to say that the Scout sent across should be competent not only to swim or to use the raft, but he must be of use when he gets there and, for example, he must be able to tie the right kind of knot to make fast the rope which will eventually be in his care and keeping.

Let us first consider the various methods of crossing, and I would say something about all of them which is very obvious but often overlooked. It is virtually impossible to throw a heavy rope in whole or in part across a stream or over the bough of a tree, and it is wasteful of time and energy to try to do what is impossible. Therefore, a necessary part of your Pioneering equipment must be a sufficiently long line which can be carried, thrown, or projected across a stream. This line, in turn, will be attached to a heavier line and this in turn may be attached to the main rope or bundle of spars you wish to send across. Therefore, all practice at getting a rope across a stream should be concerned with getting a light line across. I believe that the best type of thing for this purpose is codline, which is preferable to sisal or cheap string.

Now to the individual methods:—

Swimming or Wading Across

The Scout must be a competent swimmer and the Scouter must be satisfied that there are no hazards in the stream. The simplest method is to fasten the codline round the waist of the boy with a bowline—not round the neck or the leg where it can become tangled, and not with any kind of slip knot or in a position where it will impede the swimmer.

The Raft

There are two simple types of raft which are worth considering in this regard. The Oil Drum Raft will take A Scout across and will keep him above water. In this case I think it is more sensible to attach the line to the raft rather than to the Scout. (If he falls overboard at least you will get the raft back!) The other raft is the type which will do no more than give extra support to the swimmer, and this I would advocate using in choppy water or a swiftly-flowing stream.

The Otter

If the stream is flowing very quickly we can use this method of getting a line across, but it pre-supposes that there is someone on the opposite side of the stream.

I have recently discovered "The Otter" and I found it by looking through the original Deputy Camp Chief's Handbook published as long ago as 1921: I obviously should have looked there before.

The illustration on the next page makes clear how to construct the apparatus. If you do not possess a couple of picks then you can improvise something that is heavier at the bottom than at the top and which will serve the same purpose. The action of the current in the stream is used to move the apparatus across the stream by acting obliquely against it, but the device does not work successfully unless the stream is travelling at four miles an hour or more.

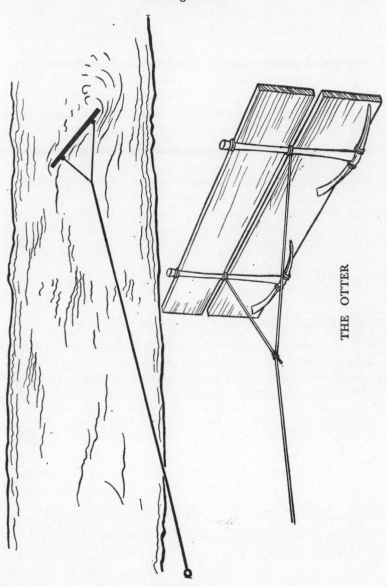

THE OTTER

Incidentally, if you are not sure how to find the average speed of a stream here is a way:

Drop a cork or a chip of wood into the water and time it over a measured distance of ten yards. This gives the speed of the surface of the stream in yards per second, and I am reliably advised that four-fifths of this figure is the average rate of flow of the stream as a whole.

To return to the Otter: You will see that it is made of two planks lashed together and weighted by means of two picks. It should be kept at an angle of about 55° to the current and the angle is obtained by securing the Otter to the swinging rope by means of a bight about three times the length of the otter. The swinging rope should be twice as long as the width of the stream.

I am sure it will be new to most of you, so have a go at it and see how you get on.

The Heaving Line

It just is not possible to throw a line any appreciable distance without a weight on the end of it. Even a life line needs a knot or a cork to give it direction of travel, but with a heaving line we can use something much heavier than we would dare to use for a life line. The Lob Stick is as effective as anything but, in fact, you do not often need anything so elaborate; a heavy piece of wood which is easy to throw will do; an old cricket ball with a hole bored through it and the line taken through the hole and secured is ideal. In this latter case I suggest you do not merely use a stopper knot, which is liable to work back through the hole, but take the line through the hole and bring it round, making fast to the standing part with a clove hitch or a round turn and two half hitches.

The most elaborate knot to use on the end of a heaving line is known as The Monkey's Fist, and you can find this in many books. This is all right if you are going to keep it there permanently, but it takes too long to tie when you are actually on the job.

It really is most important that the Scouts in your Troop learn how far they can heave a line and that they do so before they have to use it in practice. For getting a line across a stream accuracy is not so necessary as it is when throwing a life line, but they might just as well learn how to throw accurately and how to coil the line so that it does not tangle or to lay it out in open coils in front of you rather like a snake. Whichever way you use, do practise and learn exactly the limitations of your throw. If you are six feet short when you throw you might just as well be sixty feet short. You must know that your heaving line will get across to the other side, and if you know that it will not then you must use another method.

The Ballista

This is illustrated in "Pioneering for the Patrol" and consequently is not reproduced in this book. This is good fun and very satisfactory, but it does take some time to fix up. I would strongly advocate the cricket ball method for the ballista because, thrown from a cup, it holds it firmly but not too tightly and you will get the best value in length from the effort the ballista is making on your behalf.

The Bolasse

The theory here is that with great skill and a little luck (and I personally have never had enough luck to

succeed) you use this South American Goucho weapon
and cast it with a heaving line attached into a tree on
the other side of the stream.   It is a very simple apparatus: three light lines of four feet in length, one end of
each tied together and the heaving line fixed to this
joining point.   The opposite ends of the three lines
have weights fixed to them.   I think three cricket balls
would be too heavy but three stones or lumps of lead
with holes through them would be ideal.   Whirl it
round and round your head, aim it at a tree in the
distance, and let fly.   It should wrap itself round a
branch and give sufficient strength to enable someone
to use the line to pull themselves across.   I think it
is tremendous fun, but try it for yourself, and if enough
of us try then surely someone is bound to be lucky sooner
or later.

The Bow and Arrow

Particularly the modern steel bow, is a very effective
way of getting a light line to carry a much greater distance
than one can hope to throw it.   A bow and arrow,
therefore, might form part—if unexpectedly to those not
in the know—of your Pioneering equipment.   Incidentally, do have a safety cap on the point of the arrow or
make sure that the point is blunt, otherwise you will
soon run out of volunteers for being the first man across.

Finally, a tip which may be peculiar but which I
think is worth experimenting with: I find with a lob
stick that I can throw it further by having my back to
the line of flight and throwing with two hands backwards
over my head.   I learned this by finding that I could
throw a football backwards over my head much further
than I could throw it forwards. However, I am not

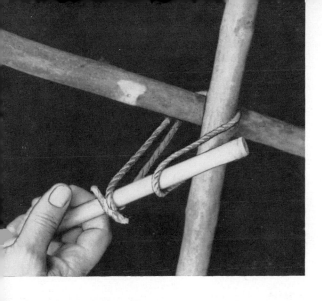

1. Strop and Turning Bar at start of operation.

TOURNIQUET LASHING

2. Tourniquet Lashing in action. (one ↑ turn short of finish).

3. Operation Completed—note fixing of Turning Bar.

←

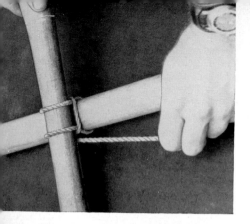

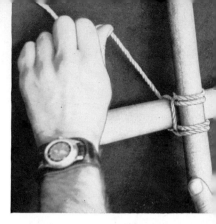

1. First set of Lashing Turns and start of first Frapping.

2. Second Lashing Turn.

SCAFFOLD LASHING

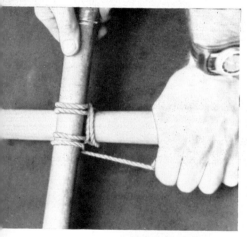

3. Two Lashing Turns and start of second Frapping Turn.

4. Complete.

5. Complete (showing ← underside).

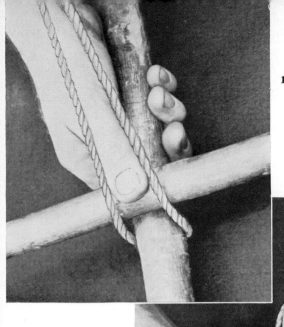

1. Showing Bight of Lashing Rope at start of operation. ←

2. Start of first set of Lashing Turns. Note how the rope is kept free of overlap. →

JAPANESE LASHING

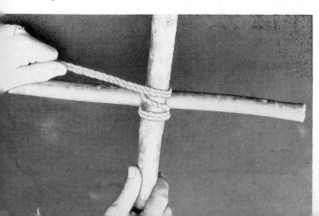

3. Completion of first set of Lashing Turns.

4. Doubled Rope divided to start Frapping Turns.

5. Start of final reef knot.

6. Lashing Complete.

7. Lashing Complete (showing under

1. Start of Operation. →

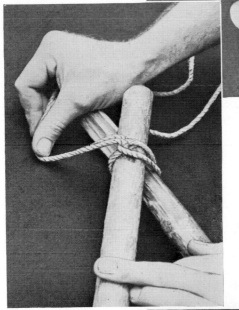

FILIPINO
LASHING

↑

2. The First Take-off —note direction in relation to bight.

3. Two Turns Completed. →

4. Changed direction of
   Lashing Turns.

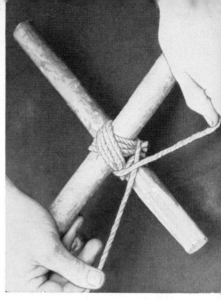

5. The Division and Take-off
   for Frapping Turns.

6. Finished Lashing.

7. Finished Lashing.
   (showing underside).

1. Four Pole
   Sailmaker's
   Lashing.

   Demonstration
   Board to Show
   Starting Process.

SAILMAKER'S LASHING

2. Four Pole Sailmaker's
   Lashing Complete.

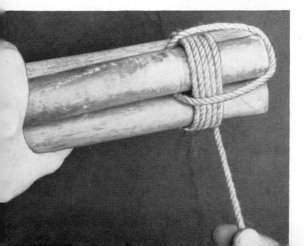

1. Sailmaker's
   Lashing.
   Later Stages.

   (See Sailmaker's
   Whipping for
   Early Stages).

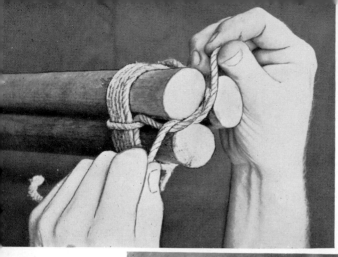

2. Starting the
final reef knot.

3. Finished Lashing
Spars opened to
Tripod Position

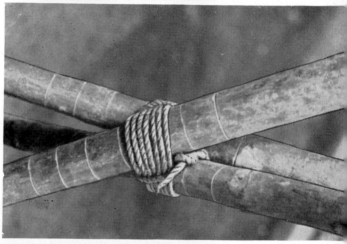

4. Finished Lashing.

Another View.

altogether convinced that this applies to everyone, but it will not take you very long to find out if it applies to you.

All I have said in this chapter seems to me to be good out of door activity on its own and there should be a great deal of fun in practising these things; and none of them require very much gear. They could well form the subject for an Inter-Patrol Competition, having the same target or "Aunt Sally" and gaining points for accuracy and for throws of the right length. I hope that here, if nowhere else, I am giving you something which you can use quite apart from its association with Pioneering as such. Scouter golfers might try a five iron!

5

CHECKING THE DEPTH

ANY Pioneering apparatus which is going into the water and which is going to rest on the bottom of a stream or pond presents problems and possibilities that are often overlooked. There are really two main problems on which I want to offer you some guidance:—

1. Taking soundings so that when, for example, a trestle is put into the water the top of the trestle is the height above water that you require it to be, and

2. When the water is deep, making sure that the apparatus you put into it will stay at the bottom and not float to the top.

There is not a great deal to say about the second problem except to stress how important it is to remember that it is a problem. In my experience, if the water is more than five or six feet deep the problem is bound to arise and therefore it is essential to have available some heavy material which will sink so that you can lash this to the bottom of the trestle or sheer legs. One of the simplest methods is bricks or rocks in a sack, not a very old sack which will rot and release the weights and, in any case, a sack is no use if the bridge has to last for weeks on end. It is possible to lash bricks or rocks to the trestles and if you can find rocks with holes in them it makes the process much easier. Metal taken from the junk yard I have referred to in other places in this book may prove satisfactory, but the important thing is to realise that you must fix something to the spars to hold them to the bed of the stream.

An attendant problem (and you may have to cope with both at the same time) is that if the bed of the stream or pond is muddy (and the Gilwell bomb hole is a very good example of this) you may find it difficult to get the spars down to a firm bottom and as the apparatus is used the spars sink deeper and deeper, thereby throwing the roadway or whatever it is completely out of alignment.

The only suggestion I can offer here is that you nail (and I mean nail, as lashing is not satisfactory) wide short planks of wood to the bottom of the spars which are going into the water. You really need something about 18 in. square or 18 in. in diameter if you prefer.

The point to remember is that you cannot put on the weights or the planks after you have built the bridge (unless you want to go skin diving) so you have to test the bottom of the pond, or stream, before you start building and then decide what action to take.

Taking the Depth

To return to the question of taking the depth: there are certain routine things to be done, whatever method you use, i.e.

1. You must decide where you want the trestle or sheer legs to be.

2. Having decided that, you must measure the distance from the bank along the top of the water to the point of entry.

3. At the chosen point you must measure the depth.

The Gilwell Depth Recorder

Illustrated here is a new and I believe original piece of apparatus which is good fun to use and has the merit (if it is a merit) that no one has to go into or on the water: it can all be done from the bank. As you see it is a very simple method. It requires a length of line, and I think codline is the best, and this will be marked so that it can be used as a measure. You then need a floating box or log which can be pushed into the stream and floated out; and on to this float you fix a simple pulley or roller so that the weight which you are going to lower on to the stream bed can move freely and thereby give the accuracy. Then, of course, you have a line fixed to the box and this also must be marked so that when a reading is taken you know exactly how far away from the bank is the point where you measured the depth. The purpose of the Scout stave, which can be any stick, is obviously to make sure that you take all the measurements from exactly the same starting point.

An improved model will have a continuous line from one bank to the other so that the apparatus can be manoeuvered accurately to any point on the measuring line.

Using a Raft

A simple oil drum or tarpaulin raft is a perfectly feasible way of taking the depth. I would advocate a

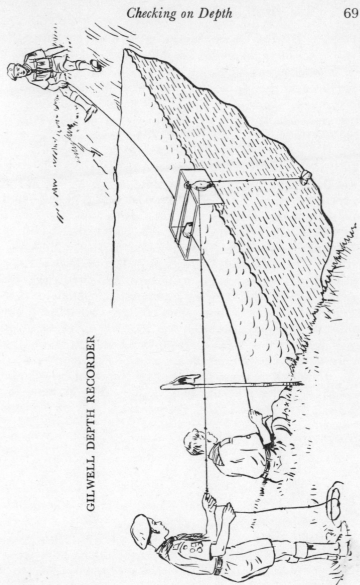

GILWELL DEPTH RECORDER

fixed line right across the stream, marked off in feet so that when you are taking the depth you know exactly how far from the bank you are. By leaning over the side of the raft you then lower a string to which is attached a heavy weight, and this string also should be marked in feet and inches so that you can know the exact depth at any point.

Using a Fishing Rod

All coarse fishermen know the importance of sounding the depth of the stream they are fishing in and they use their ordinary equipment, i.e. a rod, a line, and a reel. Instead of using a baited hook, when they are plumbing the depth they fix a lead weight which is called a plummet so that they can gauge the depth and adjust the float accordingly. If the angler can do it, then we can do it, using precisely the same equipment and method. The slight difficulty from our point of view is that we need to be a little more accurate than does the angler, because he is going to fish over an area and we are going to build a trestle on a particular spot. If you run a line across the stream then you can lower the fishing line against a definite mark and not just vaguely drop it into the stream.

Swimming

If you have no apparatus and no time to build a raft then you can get the depth by swimming and lowering a line from whatever point is indicated by those watching on the bank. This is a rather slap-happy method, but it is infinitely better than no method at all.

If you have been asking yourself why all this is necessary the answer is that if you are going to build a piece of apparatus you not only want it to serve a purpose but it is also important in Scouting that the Scouts have some pride in the appearance of the thing they have created. A trestle bridge which looks as though it has come from a section of a switchback railway at an amusement park may be entertaining, but it is not efficient and you cannot be proud of it. The only way I know to get the roadway level is to take soundings before I start and then to design the trestles in such a way that when the roadway is put on them it really is level. Quite apart from efficiency, though, this taking of depths is simple elementary Pioneering which the youngest Scout can take part in, enjoy doing, and learn at the same time. If we give sound basic training at the outset then we are establishing good practices and principles which may bear real and successful fruit in the future.

6

THE TOOLS OF PIONEERING

WHILST a great deal of simple Pioneering can be done without tools and all that we need to do is to lash and to anchor, if we are going very far along the Pioneering trail we shall find that tools become more and more necessary and that they add an extra spice of interest for the boy.

Many of the tools I shall refer to will be familiar to you and in the main they will be the most essential ones, but others you may not have heard of before. I do not advocate that you should rush out and buy them all but if they come your way seize upon them, learn how to use them, and don't let them end up in the Group's jumble sale.

The Spade or Trenching Tool

I have put this at the top of the list because I believe it is vital to have some instrument with which you can make the essential hole which helps the spars to be gripped by the earth. The spade is also useful when ground has to be levelled, when we want to remove turf in order to protect an area on which we are going to build, and it is essential for a Dead Man's Anchorage. Incidentally, we should certainly remove the turf if fire is involved in any project as, for example, a Beacon Tower. Yes, a spade is a very useful tool and some sort of digging instrument is a necessity.

The Axe

I put the hand axe very high on my list of necessary tools. We may well have to point pickets and that is a tedious performance if you try to do it with your teeth, although I suppose the Beaver Patrol is trained to be the exception!

I always use a hand axe for cutting rope as it gives a cleaner cut and therefore a better end for whipping than does cutting even with a sharp knife.

I do not consider that this is the right place to consider how to use an axe, but I would remind you that it is at one and the same time a useful tool and a dangerous weapon and all the safety rules which we know and I hope explain to Scouts during their training for Second and First Class Axemanship apply equally in Pioneering, in particular masking the axe when it is not in use and keeping it sharp and in good condition.

The Saw

I suggest a Bushman's Saw for preference, but whatever type you have it should be in good condition and kept sharp. Possibly you will need a saw to cut off the jagged end of a broken spar, to shorten a spar which is too long and adaptation does not prove possible, and certainly on occasion you will need it to trim undergrowth and overgrowth near, for example, the bank of a stream.

The Billhook or Bagging Hook

Great Britain provides an infinite variety of these tools. I believe it is true that every county has one model which it swears by and, indeed, quite often the rural community swears at any other type. I do not wish to enter into traditional controversies, but merely to say that a bill or bagging hook is a very desirable thing in relation to Pioneering and so long as it cuts undergrowth, grass, bracken, and nettles, I do not think it matters very much whether it is a Wessex pattern or an Icelandic pattern.

Now we come to some of the tools with which you may not be familiar. I have illustrated them for you but they may need a word of explanation:—

The Cant Hook

This is a heavy, rather ugly tool and its purpose is to help move heavy logs from one point to another as we often need to do in Pioneering, sometimes to get them out of the way and sometimes, as for a Lifting Bridge, to get them into position, and the same applies with a Log and Picket Anchorage.

The cant hook is a semi-mechanical lever. The principle is a lever spar and at the working end there is a sharp point known as the 'lip' which digs into the side of the trunk and a curved hook ending in a sharp point set at right angles to the line of the hook which digs into the side of the trunk opposite to the lip. The apparatus enables you to take a firm grip on a fallen tree trunk and, by working the lever, to manoeuvre the trunk as you may wish. The limiting factor is simply that the diameter of the trunk may be greater than the

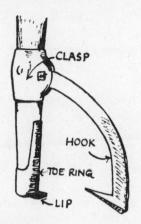

THE CANT HOOK

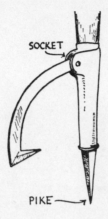

SOCKET

PIKE

THE PEAVEY

maximum distance between the lip and the point of the hook, but otherwise it is a very effective tool.

The Peavey

This is a logical development of the Cant Hook. It is identical in action except that in place of the lip of the cant hook there is a sharp spike as a continuation of the lever spar and this spike is dug into the top of the trunk you wish to move and then the hook operates in just the same way as on the Cant Hook.

I think it is obvious that, in theory at any rate, with the Peavey you can grip a log that has a diameter twice the size of the opening between the point and the hook.

The snag I have found with this tool is that with very hard woods such as oak it is a very difficult job to get the point embedded sufficiently far into the trunk to hold.

THE PULP HOOK

The Pulp Hook

This is a piece of equipment not used very much in this country but I have seen it often abroad and, particularly for soft woods, it is a very useful tool for moving logs.

TELEGRIPS

Telegrips

These are comparatively modern although we have used them at Gilwell for nearly twenty years. It is a tool of the forest and the illustration shows how it is used. It is really a two-sided Cant Hook. One of the things that Scouts enjoy is finding that with a minimum of effort four Scouts can move a really heavy log. Incidentally, you do need to use Telegrips in pairs; there is not much you can do with one set.

The danger point in using them is when you engage the hook and lift the log from the ground. Make sure that the points of the hooks are buried firmly and make sure also that the initial lift is done by the Scouts with their knees bent. Learning how to lift heavy weights is important, otherwise strains are probable and they are easily avoided if we give proper training.

The Lever

Two scouts intelligently operating a lever can learn how to turn a log round on its axis and thereby manoevre it into the exact position where it is required.

THE LEVER

ROCKING

Rock 'n' Roll

This leads me to say a word about Rocking and Rolling, not in the dancing sense but in the Pioneering context. If a Patrol of Scouts strain at a fallen log of any size and try to roll it they will have to make a terrific effort to get it moving at all but, no matter how big the log is, if they will line up with their hands on the log as the drawing shows and then begin very gently to rock it backwards and forwards, the moment will come when the log will want to be rolled over. I believe it is one of the most satisfying things, particularly for a young Scout, to learn what a great deal of power he and his companions have if it is harnessed and used in the correct way. This is something you can try on a hike whenever you come across a fallen tree, and I think you will be astonished at how quickly the trick is learned and how effective it is.

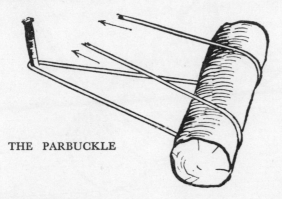

THE PARBUCKLE

The Parbuckle

This is another method of moving heavy timber. You don't really need to have a stake in the ground as the artist has shown, although it is perfectly correct to do so; someone standing on the bight of the rope serves the purpose just as well.

I think parbuckling is a four man job; one standing on the bight, one standing on each pulling rope and one to watch the operation.

The Gun Tackle

This is an exciting method of moving a log a good distance and the speed you can achieve is amusing if you can get a Patrol working efficiently as a team, but don't use the gun tackle on a down-hill run or you will end up by needing gun carriages!

Finally, about all these things: Don't wait until you get into camp or into the woods to learn about them and to practise. Some of these things can be done

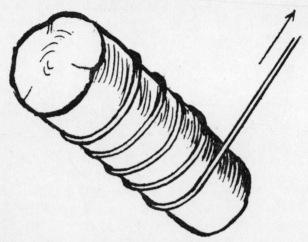

THE GUN TACKLE

in the Troop Room and all of them can be done on waste
ground, and they are all things worth learning in advance
of the need actually to use them. They are good Troop
Meeting programme material for Scouts, Senior Scouts,
and Rover.

7

SAFETY IS NOT TIMIDITY

THE greater the height the further it is to fall: the more complicated the structure the more things there are to go wrong and to become weak. The greater the risk the greater is the Scouter's responsibility for eliminating unnecessary risks. It is worth remembering that you do not produce men of good character by killing them off in childhood or adolescence. Our training must always have an appearance of adventure and on occasion must be adventurous, but the more adventurous it is the more trouble we must go to in order to eliminate the avoidable risks.

I have listed a number of points that I know need watching and which are often overlooked: there are others, but I do want to impress the need for every care in Pioneering.

1. *Testing the gear.* I have written already about checking the condition of ropes, and this is particularly necessary with the main rope of any structure, e.g., the foot rail of a Monkey Bridge and, perhaps most vital of all, the runway of an Aerial Runway. Equally, we need to be satisfied that the guys and lashings are of good quality and are in good order. Spars are bound

to deteriorate; whether they are treated or untreated their life is limited and the greater the strain that is going to be put on a spar the more satisfied must we be that it is still secure and will not let us down, e.g., the sheer legs at the downward end of the Runway.

2. *Insecure Anchorages.* Even if the spars, ropes, and lashings are absolutely first class most Pioneering projects —and in fact I would say all except rafts—depend in some measure on the way they are secured to the ground. I have seen magnificent sheer legs guyed with flimsy string because that was all that was left but, in fact, it would have been safer to use the string for the sheer lashing and the lashing for a guy. There is a long chapter in this book on anchorages, and the point I want to stress here is the vital necessity of giving training in anchorage quite separately from training in Pioneering as such. If I can take the analogy of learning to play the piano, the project is the tune and the anchorages are the scales, and in Pioneering you need to learn and practise the scales as in music. Again a reminder: The type of anchorage must be related to the soil conditions. What is good in heavy clay may be quite unsuitable in sand or chalk.

3. *Failure to protect open-ended hooks.* This is technically known as "mousing." Any hook over which a rope can be slipped can just as easily spill the rope if the conditions become in favour of spilling. An unmoused hook supporting, for instance, a bosuns chair on an aerial runway is the kind of hazard we must learn to avoid. A mousing must not only be there but must be firm and tight and almost incapable of being pushed off by the action of the rope against it.

Some years ago we experimented—not on a bosun's chair but on hook mountings that were under less strain —with extended rubber and ring mousings. These we found quite satisfactory and just as firm as a rope mousing provided we renewed them from time to time and did not allow the rubber to become perished.

4. *Failure to heel in butts.* You build a tower or sheer legs and put them up in the height of Summer on hard-packed ground. They are well made and yet they collapse. How can this happen? It can happen only because we failed to realise that when under strain there was not enough friction between the butt of the spar and the surface of the ground for the two to stay together. So a vital piece of Pioneering equipment is a small spade or a trenching tool to enable us to take off the top spit of ground to accommodate the butt of any spar which is to be erected in an upright position, so as to give the butt something to bite against. You don't need to dig a pit or even a hole: about 4 in. is adequate.

5. *Failing to watch for deterioration.* This is the kind of things that happen: A Patrol builds something; the Scouter watches them build it and is satisfied that what they have built is correct and in perfectly good order, and still an accident happens. There may be a dozen reasons for this; perhaps the anchoring picket has worked loose; perhaps a block and tackle has started to slip; perhaps a mousing has worked loose; perhaps a lashing has frayed. The good Scoutmaster and the good Patrol Leader continue to watch all the time the apparatus is being used and periodically a quick spot check is made of the vulnerable points. Anything tends to wear with use; very few things become better or stronger; ropes stretch, spars wilt, and all the things I

mentioned can happen unless we are constantly on the look out to correct faults as they occur and we make sure each time the apparatus is used that everything is secure.

6. *Overloading.* I am the last to want to curb enthusiasm and enjoyment, but sometimes when I see a well built Monkey Bridge which is perfectly capable of carrying three or four Scouts at one time, suddenly loaded with the whole Troop—perhaps for the purpose of a photograph—I shudder to see the safety margin melting away and a strain placed on the bridge which it was never designed to take.

7. *The mis-use of apparatus.* Again, it is difficult to curb enthusiasm. Trying to tip over a raft, for instance, is good fun and little harm is likely to be occasioned, but when you make a rope bridge and four Scouts on it start it swinging to and fro, then the strain becomes immense and something is liable to give way. We must realise that any movement and certainly any exaggerated movement produces a degree of strain that is many times that experienced when the apparatus is used normally.

Quite deliberately I have not attempted to set these potential dangers in any order of priority, but I am satisfied that I have given the main causes of unnecessary accidents, and it is your responsibility as a Scouter to be constantly on the alert, to exercise firm discipline if it becomes necessary, and to withdraw defective apparatus from use as soon as you are aware that it is defective.

This is all part of being prepared as a Scouter. We must think ahead, not morbidly because we are afraid that something will happen but so that we can be absolutely certain that nothing will happen. To those who decry safety first I would say that the opposite of safety first is inevitably safety last or no safety at all. The more thorough you are in your care the more adventurous can be the Pioneering projects that you can with safety and profit build to use: it is when you discard safety that it becomes impossible to adventure and to make any Pioneering progress.

8

USING JUNK

IF YOU have seen the splendid Senior Scout Film, "Accent on Adventure" you may remember the shot of the Scout who appears to be shooting rapids in a strange boat made out of a bit of corrugated iron. I remember it well and always shall. Now I don't suppose for a minute that this Scout, or any Scout, deliberately goes to a builder's merchant and purchases a new piece of corrugated iron roofing. What I hope and believe happens is that a Scout comes across a piece of junk corrugated iron and immediately thinks "What can I use this for?"

One exciting approach to Pioneering that I want to advocate is the frequent asking of this question. You see something that has been discarded or you are offered something that at first you think you do not want, or perhaps something peculiar is left at the end of a jumble sale and you ask yourself, "What can I use this for?" never "What on earth am I going to do with this and how can I get rid of it?"

It was thinking along these lines that led me many years ago to devise a series of projects based on old farm cart wheels. With the advent of tractors in the countryside the old type of farm cart and the hay wain and many other types of horse-drawn vehicles sadly but inevitably became redundant. Many of them are still lying in farm yards and the farming community has no further use for them and are happy to give them away, often for nothing, but sometimes for a few shillings so long as we remove them from the premises.

The cart wheel has its place as the basis of almost any kind of cart and, turned on its side, as the foundation for a platformed tent which will swing back and forth with the wind. This, incidentally, is a very pleasant and restful experience. The cart wheel acts as the base for a revolving or swinging bridge, and, in fact, a pair of such wheels in reasonable condition, with a little thought and ingenuity, will lead to at least a dozen separate pioneering projects.

In "Fun with Ropes and Spars" I included a ridiculous affair which, quite reasonably I think, I called "The Thing". It was inspired by trying to find something interesting to do with an old bicycle which had long passed the stage where it was road-worthy and had no secondhand value. It was, in truth, ready for the junk heap. But my junk heap is the place I draw upon to try to build something that the junk contributes to, and so "The Thing" was born. It is a bicycle lashed to a simple oil drum raft, with the pedals used for motive power, the back wheel converted into a paddle, and the steering is affected by fixing rudder lines to the handle-bars.

I was happy and delighted when I first saw this queer thing going round the water-filled bomb hole at Gilwell, but I was not satisfied. I found that a fixed wheel cycle was much better than one that free wheeled simply because you cannot reverse with the free wheel system.　Then I thought it would help if we had extra motive power and so gears were introduced and later— because this is a friendly, brotherly Movement—we made "The Thing" into a tandem!

I know that many Troops have tried these "Things" and I know of one Troop which ran an expedition on bicycle rafts.　I hope that one day someone will have the enterprise to organise a Cross-Channel bicycle raft effort, but I think personally, I am getting a little old to enter for it.

The bicycle, then, provides simple motive power, and I have seen one used to power a water mill and, indeed to operate a pump.　I don't think it is too far-fetched to say that one can use a bicycle in conjunction with a windlass and, if you want to work hard, it is not too difficult to use bicycle power to work a dynamo and produce electricity in camp.　This will have the added merit of getting the Scouts to bed earlier than usual!

I mentioned a windmill.　Very recently at Gilwell a Dutch Troop put up a first class windmill and the basis of the moving part was the axle of an old cart: the rest they made on the spot from spars, rope, and hay, and it really worked; the sails turned in the wind; the head of the mill turned as it should and, in fact, the whole thing was most effective.

To the cynics who ask, "What is the point of building a windmill" (and one must try to answer the cynics on occasion) my answer is that the Scouts thoroughly enjoyed making it and they were immensely proud of it when they had made it, and, whilst it remained in the centre of the Dutch camp, everyone who visited Gilwell went to have a look at it and I did not meet anyone who had not enjoyed seeing this piece of ingenuity stimulated by a piece of junk.

Oil Drums

Talking of visitors to Gilwell; there is a lorry driver who comes once or twice a year and he regards Gilwell as a very strange place. The words he uses with great regularity (omitting some of the adjectives as this is a Scout publication!) I think I can quote: "This is the only place in the country where I take empty brand-new oil drums". To some places he takes empty old drums and to some places he takes full new drums and even full old drums, but only to us does he bring new empty drums. One day we will tell him the answer but at the moment we keep the fun going.

Yes, we use oil drums, and the oil companies are kind to Gilwell and send us a supply once a year at least. I think they get a little colourful and unusual advertising out of it, but it suits both of us that way.

Old oil drums are nearly always junk, but as the basis of a raft there are few things which work so well, provided that we look after them.

I give you these points of advice about oil drums:—

1. Before you use them, check them and make sure that they are watertight. A good way to do this is to fill them with water. If no water gets out then none can get it.

2. Make sure that the bungs are uppermost when you use them and, incidentally, make sure that the bungs fit. If you keep the bung above the anticipated water line you ought to be all right.

3. Discard without hesitation any drum which starts to leak. There may be some other use to which you can put it, but you certainly cannot use it for a raft or a pontoon bridge.

4. Try to have a variety of oil drums, not of the make of oil but of the size. We find, for example, that a raft made of a couple of forty-gallon drums with outriggers made of two gallon drums or five gallon drums is a very fine construction. I am not going to give you the exact formula because I want you to experiment for yourself, but generally speaking we reckon that a raft with a light wooden frame supported by six two gallon oil drums will carry a full grown man comfortably and two men if it must, but it does not like doing so. It will carry two medium-sized Scouts. In other words, six drums will support about fifteen stones in weight, and if you want a raft capable of carrying two men, eight oil drums seem to be about right. By the same token, one forty gallon drum will carry two men without any trouble. But don't take all this from me: conduct a few experiments—not so much in terms of weight per oil drum but whether a raft made of six oil drums will or will not support the Patrol Leader of the Peewits and the A.S.M. That is the kind of formula I recommend to you as being realistic and practical and is one that you can find out for yourself without too many mathematicians being involved.

Yes, oil drums are essential in my Pioneering list, and they don't take up a lot of room in a store, but they contribute to an infinite number of Pioneering purposes.

Improvising

In Scouting we have always prided ourselves on our

ability to improvise, but improvising does not mean doing without. It is much more attractive to think of improvisation as putting something (in this case, junk) to an unexpected use, a use its original designers had no conception of.

Again to the cynic. I would say that somewhere along this road we are pointing in the direction of new discoveries. A great deal of mechanical ingenuity has been achieved by what I would call "stepping out of line"; deliberately trying to be original and using an article, a substance, or a material for a use for which it was never intended.

Look at your junk carefully and think objectively and constructively about it. Perhaps most important of all, don't be disappointed if the idea you are trying out doesn't work. Not unnaturally, I only publish the successful ideas I have had. I have played with any number of complex and sometimes very interesting items that have ended in complete failure; particularly, I remember, the three dimensional runway which was supposed to operate in three distinct ways simultaneously. We used every block and spar we could lay our hands on, miles of rope, and dozens of spars; we had bruised knuckles, but we never made it work, so you will not find it in any book on Pioneering. It does not do to be disappointed because that can only lead to a point where you no longer wish to try.

9

UNORTHODOX MATERIALS

BAMBOO, unfortunately, does not grow to a useful size in Great Britain but it is one of the many things that, as an island race, we import and it is readily available in this country. At Gilwell we have been very well served by a firm called Jacobs, Young & Westbury Ltd., at Bridge Road, Haywards Heath, Sussex, and they will supply bamboo for what at the time of writing seems to me a fair and reasonable price. You will see from the prices they send you that there are two types of bamboo currently and commonly available, the tapered bamboo which runs from whatever the butt size is to almost nothing, which is all right for flag poles but not much good for stable pioneering, and the bamboo which does not taper and this is the kind I suggest you get to add to your store.

You may want to know how long bamboo will last. There can be no easy answer but if it is properly used and stored in a dry place it will last very many years and it does not seem to be susceptible to attack by insects. A word of warning, though: If bamboo snaps don't throw the broken ends on the Troop Room fire, but save them for your Guy Fawkes Party as you will not need to spend so much money on fire crackers. Bamboo explodes in a fire, as I know to my cost for I remember opening a Camp Fire in the West Indies with the familiar phrase, "As the flames point upwards" but unfortunately they came out sideways, exploding fearsomely and penetrating my blanket without any apparent trouble.

There are two advantages connected with bamboo and I advocate them strongly and urge you to include in what I hope is your developing store of equipment, enough bamboo to build at least a tower and a bridge.

The first advantage is that because the material is light it is easy to store and is ideal for indoor displays. Many Scouters must have seen the bridge which is always a feature of the pageant play "Boy Scout". Bamboo is good for display work because, being light, it can be speedily handled by Scouts.

The second advantage is that it enables quite young Scouts to build projects which would be beyond their capacity in any other material, in that they would be strained in a physical sense if using heavier material and would not have the strength to lash together 20 ft. spars of Chestnut or Larch but can easily handle 20 ft. lengths of bamboo.

There is no doubt whatever that a young Scout likes to feel that he is taking part in building something really big, and bamboo is the only effective material that I know which enables this to happen.

There are disadvantages about bamboo, but if we know about them I do not think they are too difficult to overcome. For example, bamboo is not good at taking an indirect strain. It may well make an excellent tower because the strain—assuming the tower has been properly built—can be absorbed by the structure, but it is not so good for a monkey bridge or for sheer legs used in an aerial runway because the strain is then on the tops of the spars and they are liable to fracture. If the strain is downwards or upwards bamboo is perfectly safe to use, but if the strain is sideways it becomes a dubious material to use and is best avoided.

Another disadvantage is the difficulty of lashing. Except in its natural state, i.e., freshly cut in the jungle, bamboo quickly becomes smooth and almost polished, and therefore there is very little friction content and lashing by traditional methods is ineffective. In theory, you ought to be able to make a lashing sufficiently tight to hold on any substance, but bamboo is hollow and if you pull a lashing with the utmost strength it is probable that the bamboo will give way and collapse into its centre. Experiments at Gilwell and my considerable experience with bamboo in tropical countries enables me to give you the right answer. The answer is in two parts and I recommend that you use both methods, not as alternatives but simultaneously. First, use the Japanese Lashing and the Filipino Lashing. Both these I first saw used with bamboo and they are very much more effective with this material than are the traditional Square or Diagonal Lashings. The second safeguard is to provide artificial friction, and there are several ways of doing this; a sisal whipping at the point where you wish the lashing to be is one way, although it takes rather a long time to do. We found that the speediest way is to use something like electrician's insulating tape. Put three or four layers round the areas where you wish the lashing to hold. The combination of the Japanese Lashing and the adhesive tape ensures stability and therefore success.

There is a further factor you should consider although in practice you cannot always do much about it. Bamboo grows in a fashion peculiar to itself and every now and then there appears on it what looks like a joint but is in fact a growth cycle. This is a knotty part which runs round the circumference of the bamboo, dividing two very smooth parts. If you can construct your project in such a way that two of the knotty parts come together that will give extra strength to the lashing.

Bamboo, then, has virtues not obtainable in any other material and its problems can be overcome, as I hope I have convinced you.

Steel

I can almost feel the shudders of the purists as they see this heading and I can feel the effort some of you are making to go on reading this chapter. I know that steel does not grow in the backwoods, but neither, for that matter, do oil drums and manila rope. Steel is a modern construction material which is available, and builders and civil engineers will lend it to us. The Senior Scout in particular will revel in handling it. It may be that you can get a few usable lengths "jobbed" out to you at a good second-hand price, and why should we not use a modern material and give our Scouts a chance to learn how to handle steel and the metal ties which are an essential complement in steel erection? Apart from rafts, where steel is not a very satisfactory material, almost every other item which appears in Pioneering books can be built in steel just as in wood. I am not suggesting that we abandon working in wood, but I am saying that there is no need to stop at that stage: I do not think there is any need to stop at any stage. The very word "Pioneering" means that we reach outwards and that must on occasion mean that we bring into the picture materials which have not been there in the past.

Having perhaps shocked you by mentioning steel, let me talk about something else that is relatively new.

Polythene Bags

I do not in this book recommend these as a means of keeping moths out of your uniform because I hope you and your Scouts wear uniform sufficiently often to give no moth the opportunity to settle, but I recommend them as an interesting and effective way of providing buoyancy for a raft or pontoon bridge.

These things do work. They are not likely to have a long life, and polythene bags and mountaineering boots are not a happy combination, nor are long-nailed bare feet, but long nails are something a Scout should never have.

It should not be necessary for me to explain how to blow up and secure a polythene bag, but one piece of advice I can give you is that cheap polythene bags are no use in Pioneering; they are liable to be what the trade calls "seconds" and in all probability have tiny flaws which you may not be able to see, but which water will rapidly discover.

Our experiments at Gilwell with polythene bags are of fairly short duration but they have been sufficient to satisfy me that this is not just a stunt but a real proposition.

Nylon and Terylene Ropes

I have mentioned these briefly in another part of the book. They are expensive but as their use becomes more common and production methods improve it is probable that the price will drop. But they are not so expensive as to be beyond the reach of the average Scout Troop, at any rate in small quantity, sufficient to allow the Scouts to learn the properties, behaviour and snags of these man-made materials. A few pounds spent on these modern ropes, especially for Senior Scouts, will produce a fascinating comparison between traditional knots tied in traditional material and the same knots tied in nylon or Terylene rope. Having learned the differences then, the field is open to experiment and to find out which knots are the best for these new materials.

There is no space in this book and I have not the knowledge to take you very far along this experimental trail, but I commend to you two books called: "Nylon Rope" by K. Tarbuck (published by Bristol Ropes) and "Anglers' Knots in Gut and Nylon" by Stanley Barnes (published by Cornish Bros.).

The Scout Staff

It seems odd to have this mentioned under the chapter heading "Unorthodox Materials" but I think the use of the Scout staff would be new to many Troops nowadays. I know it is unsuitable in this age for parading through suburban streets, and there are few things more objectionable in a railway carriage or on the top of a bus, and the personal ownership of a Scout staff has tended to die out for these reasons. It remains, though, a splendid piece of Troop equipment and, in fact, I consider it an essential piece of Troop equipment simply because it is exactly the right size and the right material for early Pioneering training—and I am not thinking only of the making of a trestle as laid down in the tests.

There are very few projects that cannot be made, demonstrated, and up to a point used, with material the size of a Scout stave, and next to bamboo for indoor practice and demonstration, the traditional ash stave is the best thing.

I do ask you to make sure that as part of your pioneering equipment you have at least twice as many staves as you have Scouts and that you use them to give the younger boys some experience before they go out on the full scale jobs, and you encourage Senior Scouts to try out new ideas at Scout staff size first.

To round off this chapter I would say this to you: If you believe, as I believe, that Pioneering should be an adventure then you will want to experiment with materials as well as with projects which you have not previously used. One test of any activity in Scouting is surely "To what extent do we maintain interest after the principles have been absorbed and practised?" Well, one way of maintaining interest is to pioneer in the full sense of the word. I shall always be prepared to try something new. If it fails I will write it off and put it down to experience, and if it succeeds it adds a further small chapter to the art of living and the game of Scouting.

PRICE LIST OF BAMBOO POLES

Per Dozen Pieces

7 ft. x $\frac{5}{8}$ in./$\frac{3}{4}$ in. butt	9/-
8 ft. x $\frac{3}{8}$ in./$\frac{3}{4}$ in. butt	12/-
6 ft. x 1 in. butt	15/-
6$\frac{1}{2}$ ft. x 1 in. butt	18/-
7 ft. x 1 in. butt	21/-
8 ft. x 1 in. butt	24/-
12 ft. x 1 in. butt	27/-
7$\frac{1}{2}$ ft. x 1$\frac{1}{4}$ in./1$\frac{1}{2}$ in. butt	27/-
9 ft. x 1$\frac{1}{4}$ in./1$\frac{1}{2}$ in. butt	30/-
10$\frac{1}{2}$ ft. x 1$\frac{1}{4}$ in./1$\frac{1}{2}$ in. butt	42/-
12 ft. x 1$\frac{1}{4}$ in./1$\frac{1}{2}$ in. butt	54/-
18 ft. x 1$\frac{1}{4}$ in./1$\frac{1}{2}$ in. butt	114/-
18 ft. x 1$\frac{1}{2}$ in./1$\frac{3}{4}$ in. butt	126/-

TAPERING BAMBOO POLES

12 ft. x $\frac{5}{8}$ in./$\frac{3}{4}$ in. butt	15/-
14 ft. x $\frac{3}{4}$ in./$\frac{7}{8}$ in. butt	18/-
16 ft. x $\frac{7}{8}$ in./1 in. butt	21/-
18 ft. x 1 in./1$\frac{1}{8}$ in. butt	27/-
20 ft. x 1$\frac{1}{8}$ in./1$\frac{1}{4}$ in. butt	33/-
22 ft. x 1$\frac{1}{4}$ in./1$\frac{3}{8}$ in. butt	39/-
24 ft. x 1$\frac{1}{4}$ in./1$\frac{1}{2}$ in. butt	48/-

Carriage extra

10

USEFUL PIONEERING HINTS
AND EXPEDIENTS

The Rope Tackle

YOU may have met this method of straining a rope under a variety of names. I have heard it called the Hayman's Hitch, the Harvester's Hitch, and the Wagoner's Hitch because all these occupations make use of the rope tackle and it is a very fine way of securing a load, just as it is a splendid way of taking a strain.

The rope tackle, properly used, can often make unnecessary the use of mechanical blocks although there is obviously a limit to the power of the rope tackle and the strain on the actual rope is greater than when the rope is passed through blocks.

In effect, the rope tackle is half a sheepshank. Let me try to explain how to make it and use it:—

Let us assume that we are trying to tighten the runway of a light monkey bridge. We would bend one end of the rope in which we are going to make the tackle on to the end of the rope that forms the roadway of the bridge. We would then take the short end of the tackle rope and pass it round an anchorage. Working towards the bridge, we would take a bight and throw a half hitch

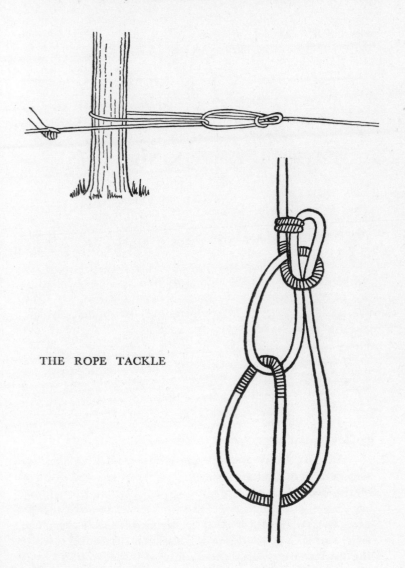

THE ROPE TACKLE

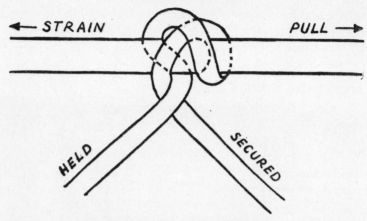

RELIEVING THE STRAIN

over it just as though we were starting to make a sheepshank but then, instead of forming the other end of the
sheepshank, we pass the running end of the tackle rope
through the long bight and tighten by pulling on the
running rope away from the bridge and towards the
anchorage. I hope the illustration makes this clear.

I would certainly expect the Scouts to be shown how
to make this tackle whilst they were learning the sheepshank because it adds great point and purpose to the
sheepshank and the two things go together very effectively.

Relieving a Strain

Where a heavy strain is being taken on a rope and it
becomes necessary temporarily to relieve the strain from
the anchorage, a rolling hitch or stopper hitch is useful.
The necessity may arise because the anchorage works
loose, or needs to be moved, or because a weak place has
been discovered in the rope under strain. The hitch
can be placed in position whilst the strain, or pull, is being

taken, and held in place. When it is required to transfer the strain, the hitch is tightened up and the strain taken by the stopper.

Using the Round Turn

One, two or three round turns around a smooth object, such as a tree, spar, or even a bundle of Scout staffs well secured, will enable a heavy strain to be eased or a heavy weight to be lowered with perfect safety. The turns are taken on top of the standing part, and, where possible, are eased from the same direction as the strain. One turn is generally sufficient, and only when a very heavy strain or weight is involved are more turns necessary.

In raising a weight or taking a strain by short pulls the round turn is of great use. Before commencing to pull, the free end of the rope should be taken round a smooth object in a complete round turn. One person then takes the end in hand, and takes in the slack as the pulls are made. It is essential to be certain that the object selected round which to put the round turn is safe before the weight or strain is thrown on it. It is quite wrong to attempt to take the weight of a heavy object or strain by simply "hanging on" and such a course is bound to place too much of a strain on Scouts.

When lowering a person over a cliff or from a window, it is essential that something in the nature of a smooth object should be placed where the rope is likely to chafe. Over a cliff a Scout staff, well anchored, or at a push some turves or even a coat should be placed where the rope passes over the edge. Out of a window a pillow, mat, or rolled sheet or blanket will do.

If the rope is taken around a post or other object with a round turn it can be paid out gradually and the person lowered carefully and evenly.

Raising Sheers by means of a Lever Spar

It sometimes happens that it is necessary to erect a very heavy pair of sheer-legs, or even a flagstaff or derrick. Frequently, this is done by means of a smaller derrick or sheers, but for most of our purposes a lever spar will be found sufficient.

A spar one-half the length of the derrick should be laid beside it, centre to centre. In the case of sheers, the butt of the lever spar will be placed between the legs of the sheers. A sufficiently strong guy is then attached to the tip of the sheers and brought back to the tip of the lever spar, to which it is attached with a half hitch only, the length of the guy between the tip of the sheers and the tip of the spar being roughly two-thirds the length of the

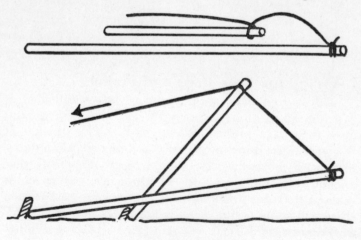

LEVER SPAR

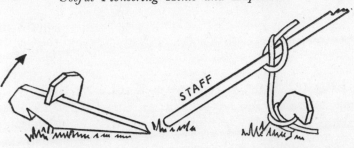

LEVERING UP TENT PEGS AND PICKETS

sheers. Foot-ropes should be attached to the butts of
both sheers and spar, or pickets knocked into the ground,
so as to prevent them sliding. Light guys should also be
attached to the tips of both to prevent them from swaying.
By hauling on the main guy the lever spar will be raised
and will lever the sheers into position. The half hitch
on the lever spar will hold if the strain is applied steadily
throughout, then when the spar has served its purpose
it will come away easily when the strain is taken off.

This will be found quite an interesting and simple
exercise in itself, and the principle of it can easily be
demonstrated with a light spar and a Scout staff.

Levering up Tent-Pegs and Pickets

More frequently than not, very great difficulty is
experienced in lifting pegs and pickets from the ground
after they have been driven in hard. The thought of
this difficulty sometimes deters people from knocking
in pickets as far as they should, with the result that
anchorages and guys are left insecure. Once it is
realised that this difficulty can be overcome easily; then
there will be no hesitation in hammering pickets in hard.
It is quite easy to remove a tent-peg by placing another
peg, or short length of stick, underneath the tip of the

peg in the ground, and levering it upwards as indicated. An alternative method which is used especially for pickets is to use a staff as a lever. A lashing is attached to the picket by a rolling or clove hitch, and the staff slipped through a marline-spike hitch so as to lever up the picket. Care must be taken not to have the line too long. Remember to fill up your picket holes before you leave the site.

To Secure a Rope to a Hook

There are various ways of securing a rope to a hook whether for purposes of suspension or of taking a strain with blocks and tackle, etc.

The usual way adopted is to make a catspaw; in the *middle* of a rope this is made by throwing back a bight in the rope, and then taking hold of the two smaller bights now formed in each hand and twisting them up separately, and finally placing the hook in the two eyes thus formed. A catspaw at the *end* of a rope should, however, be made in a different way. A loop is made and laid over the standing part so as to form two bights; the standing part is rolled round these three or four times and the bights twisted once or twice before the hook is inserted into them.

It is not realised, however, that various hitches are preferable to a catspaw. A marline-spike hitch is used where a small pull is required; a blackwall hitch will stand a heavy strain, provided the strain is constant; a double blackwall hitch holds better than either of these two hitches and is used for the same purpose; a mid-shipman's hitch is sometimes used instead, and will hold better if the rope is at all greasy.

Slings

For the suspension or transportation of heavy objects some kind of sling is necessary, and various methods are used to serve different purposes. For slinging sacks or tents, or casks in a horizontal position, all that is required is a long strop, or a non-slip loop made by a bowline. (If weights or strains are heavy, what is known as a water-bowline is preferable to an ordinary bowline, as it will not jam so tight). Spread the loop out into an oval, lay the sack across it, pass one end of the loop through the other and over the hook.

A barrel sling is used in order to sling a cask or barrel in an upright position. Stretch the rope on the floor, and place the cask on end on it so that the free end of the rope is about twice the length of the cask. Bring the free end and the standing part of the rope up over the top of the cask, and there make a simple or overhand knot. Open this knot out and pass the two sides of it over the respective sides of the cask. Finally tie the free end to the standing part with a bowline over the top of the cask.

The Boatswain's Chair

When it is necessary for a person to be suspended (not by the neck—there is a hangman's knot for that purpose!) over the side of a building or boat or on a mast for painting or repairs, or to be transported over an aerial runway, a boatswain's—or more commonly bosun's—chair is used. Different hitches are used for this purpose and are suitable for the suspension of all kinds of planks where a hanging staging is required.

A marline-spike hitch can be used, the end of the plank taking the position occupied by the marline-spike. More frequently a clove hitch is employed; make a clove

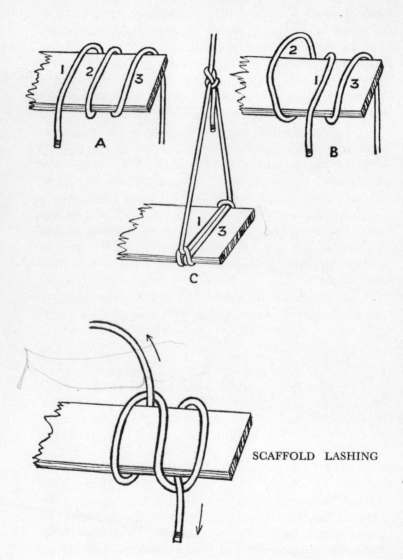

SCAFFOLD LASHING

hitch of ample size, so that when placed over the end of the plank it will hang loosely below it; upset the clove hitch by drawing the right-hand rope to the left and the left-hand to the right; turn the plank over, draw the ends up over and attach the short end to the longer with a bowline. Attach a second rope to the other end of the plank in the same way, and the chair is ready.

Probably the best method, however, is to make use of the scaffold hitch. Lay the short end of the rope over the plank leaving enough hanging down to tie to the long rope finally. Wrap the long end loosely twice round the plank. Carry rope 1 over rope 2 and place it between 2 and 3. Carry rope 2 over ropes 1 and 3 and over the end of the plank. Take up the slack by drawing on the two ends of the rope, and join the short end at a convenient distance above the plank to the longer with a bowline.

The scaffold hitch can also be used for securing a bundle of sticks or poles together.

The Lever

We often wonder how it is that, without modern machinery, cranes, winches, and so on, the Egyptians were able to move the huge blocks of stone of which the Pyramids are built, or the ancient Druids were able to lift the stones that form Stonehenge. It is probable that the only mechanical aid that the builders of Stonehenge had was the lever, which works on the same principle as the child's see-saw. When levers are used for moving logs, or prising out boulders, care must be taken to see that they are strong enough to stand the strain that is to be placed upon them. If levers are being used to lift anything from the ground, one man should be detailed to slip a roller or solid block under the object as soon as it is raised, so that those on the levers do not have to take the strain for longer than is absolutely necessary. For instance, when a large log is being sawn through with a cross-cut saw, it is frequently necessary to raise the log at the point where it is being sawn in order to prevent the saw from jamming. It is always advisable to do this before the cut is started, and not to leave it until the saw starts to stick.

Rope Ladders

Illustrated here are two simple and quick ways of making secure ladders.

One is merely a series of short spars lashed firmly to a single upright. The lashing used can be either the traditional Square Lashing or the Japanese Lashing. If you have available a piece of squared timber for the upright instead of a rounded pole it will make a more satisfactory ladder.

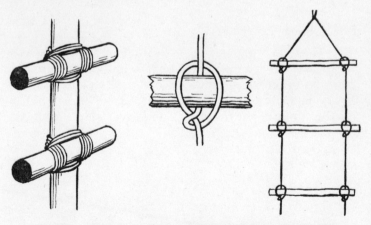

ROPE LADDER USING MARLINE SPIKE HITCHES

The second ladder illustrated is a combination of rope and short spars, using the Marline Spike Hitch which is illustrated. The vital thing to remember is that the knotted part of the hitch must be under each ladder rung so that when a weight is put on the rung the knot will work in support. The ladder used the other way round can result in the rungs slipping as the weight goes on to them.

Blocks

Several types of block are demonstrated. The choices we have in terms of material are these:—

1. All metal blocks. These are perfectly satisfactory but perhaps are not very romantic.
2. All wood blocks, including the sheaves.
3. Metal blocks with wooden sheaves. The wood must be seasoned hard wood.
4. Wooden blocks with metal sheaves.

The advantage of wood is that it is lighter than steel but its disadvantage is that it may warp or crack and wear out more rapidly.

There is a great deal to be said in terms of giving Scouts experience for trying to collect as wide a variety of types of block as possible, and this variety should apply to size as well as to different materials. Boys undoubtedly enjoy handling equipment of this kind and variety adds to the enjoyment.

In general, it is wise to use the lightest blocks obtainable, so that you can use lighter ropes, and it is worth remembering that a very heavy block has to be supported, which materially affects the whole of the structure on which you are using it.

METAL BLOCKS

SINGLE SHEEVE   SINGLE SHEEVE   DOUBLE SHEEVE
   WITH EYE   WITH HOOK   WITH EYE

DOUBLE SHEEVE BLOCK
WITH METAL SHEEVES

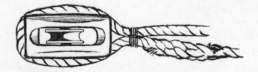

SINGLE SHEEVE BLOCKING IN
WOOD WITH METAL SHEEVE

There is not very much need in Scouting to go beyond the stage of two-sheave blocks, but multiple blocks are available and for Senior Scouts they have many points of interest.

You will notice in the illustrations that some of the blocks are drawn with eyes and others with hooks. Avoid, if you can, marrying hook to hook, but hook to eye with the hook moused is strong and satisfactory.

One final word of warning. Never use the wrong size of rope to run through a block. If the rope is thicker than the channel of the sheave it will jamb and if it is too thin it will slip off the track and, again, will jamb. Rope which runs wild through a block can easily be destroyed on, for example, an aerial runway.

The Trestle

The trestle, which is part of the Second Class Test in Great Britain, needs to be constructed accurately if full advantage is to be obtained from it. It is not sufficient merely to lash six spars together so that they look approximately like the drawing. These are the points to note:—

1. The transom, between the lashing points, should be five-sixths the length of the ledger between the lashing points. I put it this way because there is no reason to cut the spars. If there is an overlap on the transom it does not matter except from the point of view of appearance.

2. The transom and the ledger are on the same side of the structure.

3. The diagonal braces will have three ends on the opposite side of the structure to the transom and ledger and one end, nearest the ledger, on the same side.

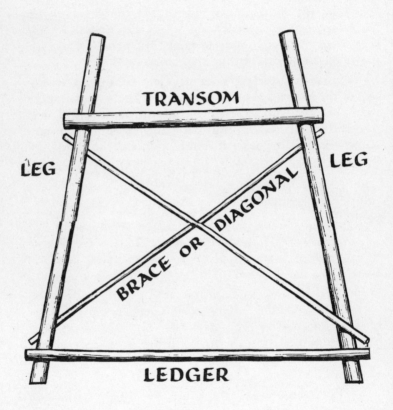

4. The lashings throughout are Square lashings except at the point where the braces cross and here a Diagonal or Filipino Lashing should be used. If you are using traditional Square Lashing begin on the transom with a clove hitch on the upright spar placed under the transom, but with the ledger the first clove hitch should be placed above the ledger, again on the upright spar. This is to ensure that the starting knot does the maximum amount of work. The transom will normally support weight from above, whereas the ledger will often have to support a thrust from below, for example, when it is placed in the bed of a stream.

Trestles can be used for many purposes but one of the great purposes in Scouting should be to get a Patrol working speedily and as a team in relation to one project.

GLOSSARY

GLOSSARY

of Terms you will meet in the pursuit of Pioneering

It does help if you know what to ask for!

ADZE   A cutting tool with a blade set at right angles to the handle. Used for shaping large timbers. A fine tool but difficult to learn to use.

ANCHORAGE   A fixed base; picket, tree, rock, or any secure object around which a rope can be tied and which will take a heavy weight or strain.

AUGUR   A carpenter's tool used for boring holes in wood.

BECKET   A rope eye for the hook of a block. Also a rope grommet used as a rowlock or any small rope strop used as a handle.

BELAY   To make a rope or line fast by winding it in a figure of eight around a cleat, a belaying pin. Also; to stop or cease.

BELAYING PIN   A pin of either wood or metal set in such places as pin rails, etc. upon which to belay a rope or secure the running rigging.

BEND, TO	To fasten a rope to another rope or some other object.
BIGHT	A loop in a rope.
BILLHOOK	A thick, heavy knife with a hooked end, used for chopping brushwood.
BLOCK	A mechanical device consisting of a frame or shell, within which is mounted a sheave or roller over which a rope is run. There are many varieties of blocks which are at times called pulleys, or when rigged, a block and tackle. the name pulley, as used in connection with a block, is a misnomer in that in this case the word pulley refers only to the sheave or roller.
BLOCKS AND TACKLE	Two blocks, through which one continuous rope has been taken, so as to form an apparatus for lifting weights, straining a rope, etc.
BOLLARD	A heavy piece of wood or metal set in the deck of a vessel or on the dock to which the mooring lines are made fast. They are also called nigger heads.
BRACE	A spar connecting two others to give support and strength.
BRACE AND BIT	A tool used by carpenters for boring holes.
BRAID	To plat, plait or interweave strands, yarns, ropes or cords.
BRUSHWOOD	A thicket, underwood, loppings of branches,

BUTT	The larger end of a spar.
CABLE	A heavy rope used in attaching anchors or in towing. A cable is also a nautical measure of length.
CABLE-LAID	Rope made up of three ropes laid up left-handed; the ropes comprising the strands being laid up right-handed.
CATCH A TURN	To take a turn, as around a capstan, usually for holding temporarily.
CHOCK, CHOCK-A-BLOCK	When two blocks are pulled so close together that no further movement in the same direction is possible.
CLEAT	A heavy piece of wood or metal having two horns around which ropes may be made fast or belayed. Usually secured by bolts or lashings to some fixed object.
COIR ROPE	Rope made from coir fibres. It is extremely light in weight but is not as strong as rope or cable made from the other common rope materials.
CORDAGE	A collective term for ropes, usually referring to cords and lines less than one inch in circumference.
CORE	A small rope running through the centre of heavier rope. It is usually found in four-strand rope, lending to it a smooth, round outside appearance.
CRINGLE	A piece of rope spliced into an eye over a thimble.

DERRICK   A single spar or post used for hoisting weights.

FAKE   A circle or coil of rope in which the coils overlap and the rope is free for running. Also "to fake down" a rope is to coil down a rope.

FALL   A rope, which with the blocks makes up a tackle. A fall has both a hauling part and a standing part, the latter being the end secured to the tail of the block. In some cases only the hauling part is considered as the fall.

FRAPPING TURNS   Turns of a rope taken at right angles to the others to tighten a lashing.

FREE END   The end of a rope which is free for working, sometimes referred to as the running end.

GAFF   A spar lashed across a mast, usually to support a sail.

GROMMETT   Eyelets made of rope, leather, metal, and other materials. Their chief uses are as eyelets secured to canvas and sails through which stops or robands are passed.

GUY   A rope to steady a load in hoisting or any rope used for steadying purposes.

GYN   An apparatus consisting of three spars lashed in a tripod, used for hoisting weights.

GYPSY	The drum of a windlass or winch around which a line is taken for hauling in.
HAFT	The wooden handle of an axe.
HALYARD	A rope for hoisting or lowering yards, sails, flags, and the like.
HAULING PART	That part of the rope in a tackle which is hauled upon, or it might be described as the end of the falls or a rope to which power is applied.
HAWSER	Any large rope, five or more inches in circumference, used principally for kedging, warping, and towing.
HAWSER-LAID	Left-handed rope of nine strands laid up in the form of three, three-stranded, right-handed ropes.
HEEL	The butt, or thick end of a spar.
HEW	To cut with an axe.
HEWING AND SCORING	Smoothing the face of a log by cutting with an axe.
HITCH	A species of knot by which a rope is bent to a hook, spar, or other rope; does not hold its position by itself.
HOLDFAST	An anchorage.
KINK	A twist in a rope.
KNOT	Strictly speaking, a knot is formed in the end of a rope. The word is loosely used to describe bends and hitches.

LASH, TO   To fasten or bind with a rope or cord.

LASHING   A rope or cord by which anything is secured.

LAY   The direction in which the strands of a rope are twisted. This may be right-handed or clockwise, or left-handed, or counter-clockwise. It also refers to the degree of tightness with which the strands are twisted, as soft, medium, common, plain and hard lay. Also used in the expressions "against the lay" and "with the lay" as denoting a direction contrary to or with the lay of the strands of the rope.

LEDGER   A horizontal spar across the bottom of the legs of a trestle.

MARLINE SPIKE   A pointed wooden or iron pin used to open the strands of a rope when splicing.

MARRY   Binding two lines together temporarily, either side by side or end to end.

MAUL   A heavy wooden hammer.

MOUSE, TO; MOUSING   To close the mouth of a hook with cord as a safety measure.

PARBUCKLE   A double sling usually made by passing the two ends of a rope under the object to be moved.

PARCEL   To protect a rope from the weather by winding strips of canvas or other material round it with the lay preparatory to serving.

PICKET	A pointed stake, post, or peg.
PURLIN	A horizontal timber resting on the principal rafters.
REEVE	To pass the end of a rope through an eye or an opening, as through a block, thimble, or bight.
SADDLE	A piece of sacking placed above a lashing to protect it from being frayed.
SCORE, TO	To make a cut in a log.
SCORING & HEWING	Smoothing the face of a log by cutting with an axe.
SHEAVE	The roller of a tackle block.
SHEER, SHEER LEGS	An apparatus consisting of two spars secured at the top for hoisting heavy weights or to act as a support.
SHINGLES	Thin tiles of wood.
SISAL	A kind of hemp, a cordage used for light lashings.
SLING	A band, loop, or other arrangement of rope for suspending, hoisting or transferring anything.
SNATCH BLOCK	A single block with an opening in one side to take the bight of a rope.
SPAR	A pole or piece of round timber.
STOP, TO	To tie down the coils of a rope.
STROP	A ring of rope used to secure a hook to an anchorage.

TACKLE   An arrangement of ropes and blocks, sometimes called block and tackle, for lifting, hoisting, or pulling.

TIP   The point or thin end of a spar.

TOGGLE   A small wooden pin made of hardwood which is inserted into a knot to make it more secure or to make it more readily and quickly unfastened.

TRANSOM   A horizontal spar across the top of the legs of a trestle.

TRESTLE   An open braced framework of timber for supporting the horizontal portion of a bridge, etc.